Biblical Authority
or
Biblical Tyranny?

Biblical
AUTHORITY

or

Biblical
TYRANNY?

Scripture and the Christian Pilgrimage

by
L. William Countryman

TRINITY PRESS
INTERNATIONAL
HARRISBURG, PENNSYLVANIA

Previously published in 1982 by Fortress Press, Philadelphia, Pennsylvania.

Published in the United States jointly by Trinity Press International and Cowley Publications, a division of the Society of St. John the Evangelist. No portion of this book may be reproduced, stored in or introduced into a retrieval system, or transmitted, in any form or by any means including photocopying without the prior written permission of Trinity Press International and Cowley Publications, except in the case of brief quotations embodied in critical articles and reviews.

Library of Congress Cataloging-in-Publication Data:
 Countryman, Louis William, 1941--
  Biblical authority or biblical tyranny: scripture and the Christian
  pilgrimage / by L. William Countryman.—Rev. ed.
    p.   cm.
  ISBN: 1-56101-088-X (Cowley: alk. paper)
  ISBN: 1-56338-085-4 (Trinity: alk. paper)
  1. Bible—Evidences, authority, etc. 2. Bible—Criticism, interpretation,
  etc. 3. Fundamentalism—Controversial literature. I. Title.
  BS480.C66   1994
  220.1'3—dc20   93-43184

Biblical quotations, unless otherwise noted, are from the *New Revised Standard Version* of the Bible, copyrighted 1989 by the Division of Christian Education of the National Council of the Churches of Christ in the U.S.A.

The quotations from Laura Bohannan in Chapter 5 come from her article, "Shakespeare in the Bush," first printed in *Natural History* in 1966 and reprinted in *Ants, Indians, and Little Dinosaurs,* edited by Alan Ternes (New York: Scribner's, 1975), pp. 203-216.

Printed in the United States of America on recycled, acid-free paper.

Trinity Press International
P.O. Box 1321
Harrisburg, PA 17105

98   99   00   4   3   2

In memory of
Bera Gray Countryman
and
Louis Countryman

Contents

Preface

The last few decades have seen a great interest in the Bible in the United States, aroused in part, I suspect, by production of so many new English translations over the last forty years. This new interest has taken many forms. In some cases, enthusiasm has outrun the careful and thoughtful consideration which the Scriptures deserve from those who claim to revere them. The objective of the present book is to discuss the most basic of all questions about Scripture: What is its relation to the believer? Christians agree in accepting the authority of the Bible; but exactly what kind of authority is it? And how do we gain access to that authority for guidance in our lives?

There have been two principal approaches to these issues in modern American Christianity. On the one hand, there are some believers who claim that they have a unique reverence for and subjection to the Bible; or to put the matter another way, they claim that their Christianity, and theirs alone, is truly biblical. These Christians imagine that the nature of biblical authority is perfectly clear; they often speak of Scripture as inerrant. In fact, however, they have tacitly abandoned the authority of Scripture in favor of a conservative Protestant theology shaped largely in the nineteenth century. This fundamentalist theology they buttress with strings of quotations to give it a biblical flavor, but it predetermines their reading of Scripture so completely that one cannot speak of the Bible as having any independent voice in their churches.

The majority of American Christians, on the other hand, belong to churches which do not make such exclusive claims either for themselves or for their interpretations of Scripture. These churches, for the most part, came to terms with historical-critical study of the Bible quite some time ago; and they have recognized that no one theological system can adequately represent the Scriptures and that the Scriptures, in turn, cannot totally determine theology. This does not mean that these churches have neglected Scripture, but it does mean that they have no simple explanation of the place of the Bible in modern Christianity.

Thus, we have had a choice between a conservative variety of Christianity which offers a simple but (as I shall show) inaccurate explanation of biblical authority and a more critical variety which sometimes has difficulty articulating positively what the Bible is and does. For many people, lay and ordained, whose interest in Scripture has been newly awakened, this creates a quandary. If we wish to study the Scriptures as the guide for being and acting as Christians, we need some notion of what the Bible is, how it works to bring God's Word to us, and how we are to approach it.

This book begins with presuppositions common to most Christians in all ages: that the Bible is central to Christianity, that it is God's Word for people in all ages, that it is authoritative. In order to explore the meaning of these presuppositions, I wish to look as honestly as possible both at what the Bible is in itself and at the ways in which it actually functions in the Christian community. The results may be disturbing at times, for I am intent on showing the Bible as it is rather than as we would like it to be. Yet this kind of honesty is what reverence for God's Word demands.

There is a half-conscious Biblicism in much of American Christianity which wants to treat Scripture as if it were infallible and, therefore, identical with God. This position is basically contrary to what the Bible reveals about itself. There is a natural and understandable human desire to have some authority available to us that would answer all questions. What God has given us, instead, is a Word which prompts more questions than it answers. In Scripture, God has uttered for us not the last word but the first—a Word designed to set us off on pilgrimage, in pursuit of that life that God has willed for us to have.

This book began life as a series of lectures given at three churches in Fort Worth, Texas, and I owe thanks to all three: Trinity Episcopal Church, whose rector, John Stanley, first suggested this topic; University Christian Church (Disciples of Christ); and Christ the King Episcopal Church. I am also indebted to colleagues at Brite Divinity School who read the manuscript and offered their criticisms: Professors Toni Craven, James O. Duke, and William R. Baird.

The revisions in this new edition are mainly of a sort designed to render the book more readable and to take account of shifts in language usage over the last twelve years. The argument of the book remains the same. My thanks to Harold Rast of Trinity Press International for encouraging me to make this new edition.

Chapter 1

The Authority of the Bible

M ost Christians take the authority of the Scriptures for granted. We do not think through what we mean by saying that they are authoritative—because we are not compelled to do so. Some Christians would be content to quote 2 Tim. 3:16: "All scripture is inspired by God and is useful for teaching, for reproof, for correction, and for training in righteousness." Probably all would wish to affirm with this verse that the Bible is both inspired and useful. Yet this does not tell us what it means that the Bible is inspired, or in what way it is useful to the faithful. These are the questions before us as we begin this study.

They are not easy questions to answer. The Bible itself makes them hard to answer, raising a variety of problems concerning its own authority. What is more, the ways in which Christians have used the Bible complicate our problems. A careful and honest examination of the difficulties both in the Bible and in our use of it is apt to offend some readers. Yet there is no other legitimate starting point. The God of truth is not served by avoiding truth. We must face the hard facts about Scripture before we can hope to hear what God is saying to us through it. For if we believe that God does speak through the Bible, we must surely believe, too, that God intends us to take the manner of that speaking seriously.

This, then, is a chapter about problems. If it seems that we have been plunged, without much warning, into the ice-cold waters of skepticism, it is only in order to wake us up to the realities of the Bible in the church, so that we can go on from here to build a positive and valid conception of the Bible's authority. The problems that we shall deal with are of two kinds: those *intrinsic* to the Bible, such as instances of error, contradiction, irrelevance, and even immorality; and those *extrinsic* to the Bible, arising not from faults within the Scriptures themselves but rather from the way in which Christians have been accustomed to using the Bible.

We shall begin with the first set of problems, since they are the more fundamental. We must, unavoidably, confront the existence of errors in Scripture—errors of all kinds. Modern American Fundamentalists sometimes insist that the Bible was totally free of error "in the original manuscripts." However that may be (and I think that they are wrong), it is a matter of little importance here and now. The "original" manuscripts were lost or destroyed many centuries ago, and such manuscripts as we do have—even the oldest ones—certainly contain their share of errors.

The Bible and Modern Science

To begin with, the Bible often describes the natural world in ways that must seem erroneous from a modern scientific point of view. The universe, as conceived by most of the Old Testament writers, was very different from what we now know it to be. They envisaged the earth as a relatively flat expanse, over which God had placed the crystalline vault of the firmament, rather like a gigantic cheesedome. There were waters above this dome (which might fall down through windows in the firmament in the form of rain and other precipitation), and there were waters below it, which welled up in the form of springs. Between earth and heaven lay the atmosphere, through which the smoke of sacrifices ascended to God's throne as a "pleasing odor" (Gen. 8:21). Since there was no outer space as we know it, an Enoch or Elijah could be taken up to God's presence in heaven without a space suit.

In other words, the whole view of the universe (cosmology) accepted by the Old Testament writers was quite different from ours; and it is reasonable for us to say that it was also quite wrong. Our broader experience, both of our own planet and of the heavenly bodies, has enabled us to have a more complete and accurate notion of how the universe is really arranged. In fact, the Old Testament point of view on cosmology was already obsolete by the time the New Testament was written, and it created great perplexity for a number of Jewish and Christian writers at the beginning of our era. By their time, Greek philosophers had already perceived that the earth is a sphere and that the celestial machinery is a good deal more complex than the older view of the universe had taken into account.

Early Christian commentators such as St. Augustine looked at the first chapter of Genesis and at once realized that it posed problems. In Gen. 1:3-5, we are told that God created light as the first of his acts of creation and that, having divided the light from the (preexisting?) darkness, he created the first day. It was not until the fourth day, however, that God created the sun, moon, and other celestial bodies (Gen. 1:14-19). How, says Augustine, can this be? We all know that it is the sun itself, in its revolution around the earth (as Greek science saw it), that makes day and night. How can there have been a day before the sun existed? Augustine's solution to the problem need not concern us here; what is important is to see that Christians of earlier ages had already discovered that the science of the biblical writers could prove erroneous in the light of later knowledge.

The same is true with regard to the scientific hypothesis of biological evolution, first clearly and persuasively set forth by Charles Darwin. This hypothesis is indeed in conflict with the first chapter of Genesis, which assumes that God created each species separately, concluding with humanity. A good many American Christians have therefore resisted the teaching of evolution in schools, and some have even concocted the pseudoscience of creationism, which they try to foist off on the public as a legitimate scientific alternative to the theory of evolution. But why should we expect the author of Genesis 1 to be accurate in matters of biology when he was wrong about even one of the most basic matters of astronomical observation? If he did not realize that the sun makes day and night, then the biblical author is scarcely going to be an authority on less obvious issues of biology.

The Bible and Ancient History

If the Bible contains errors of a scientific nature, it is no surprise that it also makes mistakes in that most slippery of areas, human history. Even in our well-documented modern age, it is often difficult to determine exactly what happened and why. The events surrounding the Japanese attack on Pearl Harbor are still not completely clear and may never be so. It is most unlikely that all questions concerning the assassination of John F. Kennedy will ever be laid to rest. The events of the past, simply because they are past, are subject to forgetfulness, misunderstanding, misinterpretation, and outright distortion. In this respect, the Bible is not different from other historical works.

There is not a shred of evidence to suggest that the world flood associated with Noah in Genesis 6-8 ever took place. On the other hand, there is plenty of evidence to suggest that this is a widespread motif of folktale that has been taken up into Scripture and treated as history. The book of Joshua presents the Israelite conquest of Canaan as the work of a brief time. Archaeology has disclosed that the conquest of the great bronze-age cities and their replacement by the simpler, iron-age culture identified with that of the Israelites was actually spread over a much longer period of time. The comparison of biblical records with other ancient records, whether preserved by recopying over the centuries or newly discovered on ancient sites, also shows that the biblical record—like all historical records—is not infallible.

We may take an example from the New Testament. Luke, in his Gospel, dates the birth of Jesus in this way:

> In those days a decree went out from Emperor Augustus that all the world should be registered. This was the first registration and was taken while Quirinius was governor of Syria. (Luke 2:1-2)

There are several problems here. To begin with, despite rather good documentation for the reign of Augustus, we have no other reference to any empire-wide census. Even though it is not impossible that Luke was the only ancient writer to refer to so important an event, it is unlikely. At any rate, we do know when Quirinius was governor of Syria (A.D. 6), and this dating of Jesus' birth brings Luke into conflict with Matthew, who places the birth of Jesus at least two years before the death of Herod the Great in 4 B.C. (Matt. 2:16). Luke (3:23) himself says that Jesus was about thirty when he began his ministry, which suggests that he, too, knew the tradition that Jesus had been born late in the reign of Herod. It seems almost certain, then, that Luke was mistaken to associate Jesus' birth with the census and with Quirinius. At the very least, there is a mistake somewhere in the Gospels, for one cannot possibly reconcile all the information.

Luke was apparently a careful author. After "investigating everything carefully from the very first," he decided "to write an orderly account" of Christian origins (Luke 1:3). Yet he proves not to be a perfect historian, by any means. We can draw another example of his difficulties from the second volume of his great work, the Acts of the Apostles. In Acts 9:23-25, he tells the story of Paul's escape from Damascus, when he was lowered over the wall in a basket. The occasion, Luke says, was the opposition of the Jewish community, some of whom "plotted to kill him." No doubt, Luke's story is generally correct, but we also have a short account of the incident from Paul himself, who blames quite another party for his difficulty: "In Damascus, the governor under King Aretas guarded the city of Damascus in order to seize me" (2 Cor. 11:32). Here, we must surely take the word of Paul, who was a principal of the incident, over that of Luke, who was not even present.

The sum of it is that the Bible is not always correct in its reporting of historical events. There are times when it disagrees with other historical sources; historians then have to decide, in each individual case, which source, biblical or nonbiblical, is mistaken. But at other times, as we have seen, one biblical account disagrees with another. Then, no matter how we argue the matter, at least one biblical report must necessarily be wrong.

Consider, for example, the accounts of Jesus' baptism in the first three Gospels. According to Matthew (3:13-17), when Jesus came to be baptized by John, John tried to dissuade him, but Jesus insisted. After the baptism itself, "the heavens were opened to him and he [presumably Jesus] saw the Spirit of God descending like a dove and alighting on him. And a voice from heaven said, 'This is my Son, the Beloved, with whom I am well pleased.'" Mark's version, however, is somewhat different (1:9-11): there is no conversation with John, and the heavenly voice now addresses Jesus directly, saying, "You are my Son...." Luke's version (3:21-22) is different again. According to Luke, John was already in prison (3:19-20) and therefore could not have baptized Jesus. (Luke does not tell us who did.) Also, where Matthew and Mark only mention Jesus as having seen the heavens opened and the dove descending, according to Luke these were both public events that anyone could have seen. Some early copies of Luke also have a slightly different version of the message given by the heavenly voice; but we are not sure which words Luke wrote.

Here, then, are some serious disagreements about the baptism of Jesus: Who really baptized him? Were the opening of the heavens and the descent of the dove public events, generally visible, or a private revelation to Jesus alone? What did the heavenly voice say and to whom did it speak, Jesus or the crowd? It is clear that all three of the reports cannot be historically accurate. Perhaps, indeed, the miraculous elements may be allowed to have appeared differently to different people. Yet there remains at least the question of John. Did he or did he not baptize Jesus? Two Gospels say yes; one, no.

Similar problems exist with another important Gospel narrative, the discovery of the empty tomb. This event, reported in all four Gospels, is rife with conflicts of detail. All our Gospels agree that the discoverer of the empty tomb on Easter morning was female, and that she saw one or more angelic beings and got a message from him or them. Beyond this, they diverge, in some cases quite widely. According to John (20:1), it was Mary Magdalene alone who went to the tomb. According to the others, she had other women with her, varying in number from one (Matt. 28:1) to an indefinite number (Luke 24:10). According to John, Mary ran at once to tell Simon and the Beloved Disciple about the absence of Jesus' body; only after that did she see the two angels. According to Matthew, one angel alone appeared, and he met the women as they first arrived at the tomb. I could easily multiply these contradictions among the parallel passages; but there is no reason to do it here, when the reader can easily do it, at first hand, by trying to write a single, coherent narrative of the event, giving equal weight to all the information conveyed by each evangelist. The task, it quickly emerges, is an impossible one.

This is not to say that the whole story of the discovery of the empty tomb is a fiction. The experienced historian knows that a source may be mistaken in many matters of detail and still correct in others or in the general run of its narrative. Rather, it is essential to see that the biblical writers are fully capable of making errors of historical fact, even in those narratives that touch upon the most central truths which they hoped to convey: the divine sonship of Jesus, in the case of the baptism; the resurrection of Jesus, in the story of the empty tomb.

At this point some readers will protest that none of this makes much difference. Is not the message of the Gospel a spiritual one? Of course, the writers of the Gospels were not careful about mere details of fact; those were not essential to their message. But in matters of faith, of understanding, of morality—in these the Bible will surely be found to be a reliable, even an infallible guide. The past is past; we want to know what the Bible has to say to us here and now. Accordingly, these readers will not feel that I have raised any real problems as yet.

Problems of Belief and Morality

Yet there are problems of another kind, too. The Bible is not only fallible in matters of science and history but also capable of contradicting itself in matters of faith and morality. Take, for example, two parallel passages in the Old Testament. The first is 2 Sam. 24:1: "Again the anger of the Lord was kindled against Israel, and he incited David against them, saying, 'Go, count the people of Israel and Judah.'" This passage is full of difficulties in and of itself: Why should a census be so grave a sin as to deserve the terrible plague with which God subsequently punished Israel (24:10-25)? And if it was a sin and God intended to punish them for it, why did he put it into David's mind to take the census in the first place? Yet it is not these problems which I wish to discuss but a slightly different one.

This problem is created by the existence of a parallel passage in 1 Chron. 21:1, which reads, "Satan stood up against Israel, and incited David to count the people of Israel." Here, the action ascribed to God in 2 Samuel is now attributed to Satan. From our later Christian point of view, it seems fairly easy to distinguish between God and Satan. Why could the biblical writers not agree? The truth is that two quite different theologies, two contrasting modes of belief, lie behind these parallel passages. In the earlier passage (2 Samuel 24), the author assumed that God, when angry, might very well act like an angry human being. Among other things, God might entrap the object of his ire into some action so flagrantly illegitimate as to justify vengeance. Much later on, when the author of 1 Chronicles revised this story for inclusion in his own book, his theology no longer countenanced such an image of God. Instead, the religion of the day attributed such entrapment to a member of God's court, a kind of celestial prosecuting attorney known as "Satan," the "Adversary."

But what is the modern reader to make of this confusion or contradiction of theologies? Perhaps there is some way, theologically, in which both statements can be acknowledged as true, where God can be seen as responsible for the acts of the Satan or even, as our authors might seem to suggest, as identical with the Satan. On the face of the matter, however, there seems to be a serious conflict between the two versions. Was the census the work of a malignant being? Is God, under some circumstances, cruel to God's people? Or is such evil the work of a lesser being, to whom God allows a certain freedom for the present? These are critical questions of belief, yet we find two biblical writers in conflict with one another concerning them.

Not only do we find theological conflicts here, but we also encounter some material which is theologically and morally repugnant to us. The idea that God would deliberately entrap a king into sin and then punish his whole people may seem repugnant enough—but there are even worse things in the Bible. And there are moral quandaries which, though they may be less repulsive to us, are no less threatening to our sense of ethical assurance as Christians.

In the former category belong such matters as the story of Elisha and the she-bears (2 Kings 2:23-25). This story is not read much in church, for very good reasons. It tells how the prophet Elisha was going up to Bethel when some small boys from the city jeered at him for being bald. "When he turned around and saw them, he cursed them in the name of the Lord. Then two she-bears came out of the woods and mauled forty-two of the boys." Elisha went calmly on to Mount Carmel. This appalling little tale is told without any indication that the biblical writers thought it out of character for a great prophet, a representative of God. Nor, it seems, did they think that God objected to being used in this way. If there are twentieth-century Christians who share this point of view, I hope I never meet up with them. There are some things in the Bible which we must all recognize as morally repugnant, or we shall no longer be able to claim even that we are human.

One of the most distressing stories in the whole of Scripture is to be found in 1 Samuel 15. This chapter contains the famous and much-used text: "Surely, to obey is better than sacrifice, and to heed than the fat of rams"

(1 Sam. 15:22b). Most people who use that verse, however, do not realize to what it refers. The obedience which the prophet Samuel demanded here was obedience to the command which the Lord had given through him earlier in the chapter: "Now go and attack Amalek, and utterly destroy all that they have; do not spare them, but kill both man and woman, child and infant, ox and sheep, camel and donkey" (v. 3). In other words, the seer is claiming that genocide, if divinely commanded, is ethically superior to the offering of a few peaceable sacrifices. To give his words effect, Samuel completed the destruction of the Amalekite people with his own hands. He took Agag, the king of the Amalekites, whom the Israelites had brought back as a prisoner, and "hewed Agag in pieces before the Lord in Gilgal" (v. 33).

Shall we justify genocide because it is found in Scripture? Shall we justify it because one of God's prophets claimed that God had commanded it? Would this not be to condemn God, in actual fact, rather than to justify the slaughter of a whole people? Perhaps there is some way in which this horrifying tale may not be without value for us. Yet there is no way around the difficulty. If we do not recognize the evil in Samuel's actions, we have no right to claim to be followers of the crucified Christ, who suffered his own death rather than force his way upon the world.

At the same time, I do not wish to suggest that the New Testament somehow escapes the moral difficulties of the Old, as if the coming of Christ had somehow resolved all difficulties. That is certainly not the case. There are fewer real horror stories in the New Testament, perhaps because the early Christians had little worldly power to wield. There is, of course, the incident of Ananias and

Sapphira in Acts 5, where the death penalty is dealt out for the sin of lying—only a little less savage than the fate of the rude boys who insulted Elisha. Yet the New Testament presents us with a different and more serious sort of moral difficulty, which we must now explore.

The ethics of the New Testament epistles are generally of an extremely passive sort. No doubt they were appropriate for a small, weak community that had little hope of influencing the social and political tendencies of the times. When the author of 1 Peter told his readers to be loyal and submissive subjects, it was probably good advice for people who could not have hoped to win a revolutionary struggle, in any case. But think yourself—for a moment—into the era of the American Revolution (1776) or of the Glorious Revolution in Britain (1688) and read the text in that context:

> For the Lord's sake accept the authority of every human institution, whether of the emperor [KJV, king] as supreme, or of governors, as sent by him to punish those who do wrong and to praise those who do right....Honor everyone. Love the family of believers. Fear God. Honor the emperor [KJV, king]. (1 Pet. 2:13-14, 17)

The exhortation to submission could scarcely be plainer. Yet in 1688 and again in 1776, thousands of devout Christians abrogated the plain standards of the New Testament and made their own independent decisions that ethics and loyalty to God required them to flock to the standards of revolution. In short, the New Testament may at times lay down an ethical standard that later generations of Christians will reject. Even the New Testament cannot, it seems, be an infallible moral guide.

The same kind of moral quandary arose again in the nineteenth century, when slavery came to the fore as a moral issue for Christians. The New Testament writers insist that Christian masters should observe a certain humanity toward their slaves ("Stop threatening them," Eph. 6:9), but they also exhort slaves to be faithful to their masters. Nowhere does any New Testament author condemn slavery as such; and in one place, Paul seems to treat it as a matter of complete indifference: "Were you a slave when called? Do not be concerned about it. Even if you can gain your freedom, make use of your present condition now more than ever" (1 Cor. 7:21). Many modern translations (including the margin of the NRSV) render the last clause something like this: "avail yourself of the opportunity." This is a forced interpretation of the Greek, however, and does not help matters along very much. At most, it would mean that Paul was prepared for slaves to accept their freedom if it was thrust upon them but that he did not want them to seek it actively.

The Evangelicals of the eighteenth and nineteenth centuries who led the fight against human slavery were intensely devout people, who would have been scandalized had anyone suggested that they were violating the ethics of the New Testament. Perhaps it is putting matters too strongly to say that they "violated" them. Yet they certainly did turn their backs on them in this matter. With regard to slavery, as with regard to other areas of social ethics, the moral stance of the New Testament is often passively conservative. One does not seek to change one's social or political station but rather to serve God faithfully in that station, no matter how degraded it may seem to be. Yet this New Testament ethical stance seemed inadequate in other circumstances----for example, in a world situation where Christians could (and did) actually abolish slavery as such.

Problems of this sort are not merely a matter of the Christian past; they are still with us today. The New Testament speaks of wives in much the same terms as it speaks of slaves. "Wives, in the same way, accept the authority of your husbands…" (1 Pet. 3:1). ("In the same way" here refers to the admonition to slaves at the end of the preceding chapter). Does this mean that Christians are bound forever to a position that the husband is the monarch of the home? Hardly. Many Christians still adhere to that understanding of the family, but many others do not. It will not be the New Testament that settles that conflict, any more than it settled the conflicts over revolution and slavery earlier. In the same way, some Christians are now calling for a reevaluation of Christian attitudes toward homosexuality, suggesting that Paul's antagonism toward same-sex sexual bonds (Rom. 1:27) is no more binding than his attitude toward slavery. Again, the New Testament itself cannot resolve the question. The day may well come, though no one can say with certainty, when Christians will read New Testament texts dealing with women and homosexuals just as we now read about the subject's submission to the monarch or the slave's submission to the master, scarcely noticing that some New Testament writers tolerated a form of oppression which we should think immoral to allow in our own day. The New Testament, then, can no more serve than the Old as an infallible moral guide for the modern Christian; the great questions still remain open to a degree.

The Authority of the Bible—
What It Is Not

The reader may by now have begun to wonder whether this line of argument does not threaten to undercut the authority and usefulness of the Bible completely. That is not my intent, nor is it the necessary result of this argument. Further on in this book, I shall begin the construction of a positive statement about biblical authority. But it is first necessary to see what the authority of the Bible is not. It does not consist in the Bible's infallibility, whether as a source of scientific and historical information or as a sure guide to theology and morality. One classic statement about the authority of Scripture has this to say: "Holy Scripture containeth all things necessary to salvation..." (Article VI of *The Articles of Religion*). That is a statement to which I and most Christians would wholeheartedly subscribe. I do not think there is any contradiction between that article of belief and the recognition that the Bible is also a fallible book.

The problem which so many modern readers are apt to feel at this point is not a problem raised by the Bible itself, which says not a word about its own supposed infallibility. The problem is one created by certain developments in the history of Christianity—the *extrinsic* problem of which I spoke above and which we must now examine. Most of us come to know the Bible in the context of its use in the church and in society at large. We come to it with certain preconceived notions about what it is and what we can expect of it. Most of these notions are unexamined; we have simply absorbed them from our environment, not only from our own church communities but from radio or television, the press, popular devotional literature, conversations with friends or door-to-door evangelists, and any number of other sources. All these influences create in us certain unconscious expectations. If the revelation of the Bible's fallibility threatens us, that is because it contradicts some of these expectations—which may or may not have been good ones in the first place.

There are two ways in which churches have used the Bible in the modern age that I think are creating unnecessary problems. One is the use of the Bible to *prove* that a certain variety of Christianity is better than others. The other is the tendency, especially strong in American Christianity, to claim that one or another modern version of Christianity is actually *identical* with the New Testament message. The effort to *prove* a certain variety of Christianity by the Bible is at least as old as the Reformation, when the Reformers appealed to the Scriptures as the basis for their effort to prune the excessively luxuriant growth of the medieval Western Catholic tradition. Much of contemporary religion, they argued, had little or nothing to do with the original Christianity revealed in the New Testament; some of it was even opposed to that earlier and purer faith. Therefore, the Bible must be used as a limiting factor, and the Christian religion should not be allowed to go too far beyond what it had originally been. If one could demonstrate from the Scriptures that baptism was a part of earliest Christianity, then it must remain a part of all Christianity forever. If, on the other hand, one could not prove the doctrine of purgatory from Scripture, then that doctrine must be rejected.

Scripture thus became something that it had never before been in the same sense—the foundation for all theology and ethics. It was not enough for all Christian teaching to be simply compatible with Scripture; it must be proven by the Bible. Now, the Scriptures had certainly been used in earlier ages as touchstones of true faith. The orthodox Christians of the second century and thereafter appealed to the Scriptures in their battle against Gnosticism and Marcionism. These heresies made a distinction between the Father of Jesus and the God who had created this world. The latter they regarded as evil (or at least incompetent); the former, as purely good and loving. The orthodox replied that the Scriptures witnessed throughout that these "two gods" were in fact one and the same. But in most of the great theological controversies of the first few centuries, such as the controversies over the Trinity and the Incarnation, *Scripture was not notably useful*. It raised problems about the Godhead and the person of Christ, but it did not solve them in any comprehensive way. Thus, theology had been forced to assume a certain independence of Scripture.

Even among the Reformers, this independence was not entirely lost. Luther was no Biblicist. Indeed, he was quite capable of criticizing one part of Scripture by means of another. For him, the message of justification by grace through faith was supreme; it was, in the fullest sense, *the* Gospel. If anything in Scripture, such as the Epistle of James or the Epistle to the Hebrews, seemed to contradict or limit the fullness and adequacy of God's grace for salvation, then one must reject such things. The followers of the Calvinist tradition, however, were eager to tie their theology more closely to the letter of Scripture; and the enormous influence of this tradition on English-speaking churches has meant that, in our culture, there is a certain feeling that in religion everything ought to be proven by reference to the Bible, preferably with chapter and verse.

This kind of proof-texting results in an approach to Scripture which at its worst is legalistic in the extreme. One might, for example, take the question of infant baptism, long practiced by the vast majority of Christians but questioned by certain denominations. If we agree that this issue must be decided by reference to Scripture, then we are disappointed to find that nowhere does the Bible say explicitly whether the early Christians ever baptized infants or not. Some will then call attention to the fact that those people who are specifically described as being baptized were all adults. The other side will then take note that, in a few instances, the record speaks of whole households being baptized; will not a whole household probably have included infants, at least among the slaves? And so on and on. Only a prior insistence that every article of belief must be proven by reference to the Scripture could have occasioned such diligent inquiry, in a case where it is quite plain that Scripture does not and will not settle the issue.

If we start with this prior conviction, we shall indeed be alarmed at the prospect that the Bible is fallible. If different parts of the Bible do speak different theologies (and we have seen that they do), or if the Bible is inadequate as a moral guide under altered circumstances (and the vast majority of Christians behave as if it is), then the Bible is not going to be much use for proving things. We may still use it for certain great purposes, such as the refutation of Gnosticism, for the unity of God is written from one end of it to the other. But it will not help us decide less central issues, such as the propriety of baptizing infants.

This prospect is particularly threatening to certain types of American Christianity which have carried the idea of biblical theology so far as to claim that they have no theology, no belief, no creed, except the Bible itself. Some of these groups call themselves "Bible Churches," intending to differentiate themselves from the great mass of Christians who, they think, do not believe the Bible simply because they do not interpret it in the same way as the "Bible Churches." Certain strands of the Restoration movement, too, belong in this group. For these churches, the old slogans of that movement ("the Bible and the Bible only"; "where the Bible speaks, we speak, where the Bible is silent, we are silent") have hardened into the belief that the system of faith expressed by these groups and these only is truly the voice of the Bible; all others who think that they believe the Bible are in fact mistaken. Then, too, there are groups of this sort in many other denominations and passing under many names. The claim they make to an exclusive and pure understanding of the Bible is also familiar to many of us from some preachers of the airwaves. For these people, admitting that the Scriptures are not absolutely consistent amounts to admitting that their own tightly knit systems of belief cannot truly represent the Bible. If the Bible may be wrong on certain points, their systems, too, may be false in certain respects. It is not surprising that they are alarmed at this discussion.

Yet loyalty to the Bible itself demands that we should see it as it is. We must be literalists in our first reading of Scriptures. We must not cover up the unattractive and revise the contradictory and negate the mistaken too quickly. God did not give us a summary of belief, a convenient statement of fundamentals, a list of propositions to be believed or of rules to be obeyed. God has given us, instead, the wonderfully deep, convoluted, and perplexing Bible—as rich in mystery as it is in light. If the Bible is indeed the Word of God, as I affirm, we must understand that it is the Word of God *as we have it* and not as corrected and systematized by the theological labors of any number of well-meaning, pious, scholarly people.

If, in accepting the Bible as it is, we find that we must give up using it to prove every fine point of doctrine, or that we must surrender the claims of this or that theology to be the only true representative of the biblical message, that is a small loss in comparison with what is to be gained—*the Word of God* itself in all its immediacy. It is a loss we should readily incur. Just as Christian, in *The Pilgrim's Progress,* gladly left his pack behind at the cross in order to move the more freely toward the Heavenly City, we shall abandon those preconceptions of Scripture that only prevent us from seeing it as it is. We shall embrace the real Scriptures now and try to see how God is speaking through them—warts and all, so to speak. Then we can be pilgrims toward the future God has in store for us, instead of trying to tie ourselves to our present inadequate faith and life.

Is this prospect alarming? There is no need for it to be. In this chapter, I have been calling attention to the existence of real problems within the Bible: inaccuracies, mistakes, moral offenses, uncertain guidance, and theological conflict. I have not said (and no one could legitimately say) that the Bible as a whole is simply that and nothing more. Let us return to the story of the discovery of the empty tomb. Granted that there are a dozen or more problems of detail in the four versions of this incident, does that deprive each individual narrative of its power? Consider the two women in Matthew's Gospel, hurrying to the tomb with no clear notion of what they will do when they arrive. On reaching the spot, they are confronted by an earthquake and the angel descending; he rolls back the door of the tomb to show that Jesus has *already* risen. As they run with fear and great joy to tell the disciples that the impossible has happened, that God has set life beyond death, has crowned suffering with victory, they meet Jesus himself on the road. There they worship him, taking hold of his feet in joy and wonder, for they have witnessed the full triumph of the Gospel (Matt. 28:1-10).

What if John's version is different? It is no less moving, no less full of the power of the Good News. Mary Magdalene, so distracted by her loss, cannot even believe the message of her angel but continues to seek for the missing body until Jesus himself comes to her and speaks her name. Unlike Matthew, John does not have her touch him. John's Gospel speaks of the miracle of Jesus' restoration to her—but also of the mystery of his separation (John 20:1-18). He is ours again, but he has gone beyond us, into that future to which he is bringing us, too, in the long, slow, painful way of this age.

The faults of the Bible do not compromise its truth.

> Comfort, O comfort my people,
> > says your God.
> Speak tenderly to Jerusalem, and cry to her
> > that she has served her term,
> > that her penalty is paid.

What if this prophecy of Isaiah (40:1-2) has never been fulfilled? What if it was but partially fulfilled in Jesus' resurrection? Has God's purpose for us changed at all? No, the Word of God in Scripture remains what it has always been—a Word of power. This power will save and transform those on whom it falls, now as in the past. The faults of Scripture do not hinder the Word of power; indeed, they are the condition under which that Word is spoken. We shall see that before we can hope to understand the Word rightly, we first need to understand why God has spoken in just these ways.

Chapter 2

What is Authority?

I f we suppose (as most of us do, unreflectingly) that authority means the same thing as infallibility, then it follows that the Bible can scarcely be authoritative at all. It is too full of errors and offenses. I think, however, that this is a misunderstanding of authority. If we are to talk about the authority of the Bible in a positive or constructive way, we had better be quite clear about what we are talking. The authority of the Bible cannot be something entirely different from other types of authority we have experienced. If it were, the word *authority* would not be appropriate in this discussion at all. It will be worth our while, then, to examine how we use this term and what we expect from *authorities* of all types in our lives.

The Nature of Authority

There are three basic things that we expect from any authority: 1) a sense of identity and hope, 2) a set of norms for belief and behavior, 3) some external checks on us to tell us how we stand in relation to hope and norms. It is easy to see how these elements work in terms of the family. The authority of parents is expressed first of all in the power they have to bestow identity and hope on their children. Children, to be sure, seem to have a great deal of individuality in the differing ways that they respond to their environments, but the first environment most children know is that of the family, which provides the reference according to which they begin to shape their identities.

If parents are inconsistent in giving their love, children have a corresponding difficulty in acquiring a sense of themselves. Even the newest infants need to be held and need to hear human voices addressed to them in order to live and grow. How else would we know that we are human? How else would we find reason to look forward to the future and to live into it? And as children grow, the role of the parent does not disappear but only changes, as the parents' interchange with the child becomes more verbal and intellectual and depends less on sheer physical presence.

At the same time that they are helping the child acquire a sense of identity and hope, the parents also begin the process of giving the child norms of belief and conduct. In a society as pluralistic as ours, there are many influences on our customs or mores besides those of the family, but no one can deny the role of parents, at least in the early stages of this process. Children begin by believing pretty much as their parents do, though usually without any conscious commitment to those beliefs. Matters of great importance to the parents will be of corresponding importance to the young child. The code of conduct that the parents demand is the child's only system of reference, at first, for modeling and judging his or her own behavior.

I don't mean, of course, that children automatically believe and act according to the patterns their parents would like to impose. I am a parent, and I know better than that. But even if the child chooses to transgress the norms, it is almost always the parents' norms that she or he transgresses.

Much of the time, of course, a child knows exactly what he or she is doing in overstepping the boundaries. At other times, the boundaries themselves are subtle and difficult to learn. In either case, the child requires of the parents the third element of authority: checks. Parents need to tell children many times over that their table manners are objectionable. Only so can the children tell where they themselves stand in relation to the norm of table manners. Exactly what constitutes an infraction? Which infractions are important everywhere, and which ones only in restaurants and at dinner parties? When have I succeeded in living up to the standards and when not? Norms are seldom crystal clear and almost never self-evident. Without someone to tell us when and where and how far we have gone wrong, we would never be able to live up to them.

What the parent-as-authority does, other authorities do as well, in the ways appropriate to them. The teacher, for example, does much to create the possibility of learning by helping the students to see themselves as learners and to hope that they can indeed acquire knowledge of a useful and interesting sort. The teacher must also go on to offer the students some norms of achievement, which set a goal and standard for their work. Finally, the teacher must help each individual student see where he or she stands in relation to the standards, which is also a step in moving closer to them.

On another level, a national government must perform similar tasks. It must provide identity and hope by handling affairs with devotion and confidence so that the people are willing to commit themselves to their national identity. It must express, through law, the standards of behavior which govern membership in the community. It must also check those individuals who fall short of the standards, and praise and reward those who meet or exceed them.

Authority, then, is roughly the same thing, no matter where we meet it in human society—from the family on up to the largest political unit. At each level, too, authority is capable of turning into something quite different, a destructive power which we may call "tyranny," for the sake of giving it a single name. How does tyranny differ from legitimate and proper authority? The difference between them is something I call "realism." True authority does not proceed in an arbitrary way, but acts in the interests of those subject to it, and with regard to the limitations that the world in which we live imposes on us.

Let me give an example. If a parent insists on particular table manners, it is not simply in order to impose something on the child or to bend the child to the parent's will. Rather, the parent is acting in the child's interest (so that he or she will not be ostracized by others) and with regard to the limitations of our world (the child will have to be able to use knife, fork, and spoon effectively in order to live in Western culture).

Tyranny, on the other hand, is exercise of power primarily for its own sake. A parent might discipline a child over table manners merely because it feels good to be able to exert one's power and confirm that one is dominant. Or again, tyranny may be the exercise of power toward inappropriate ends. Thus, a parent might compel a child to learn a completely inappropriate set of table manners, knowing that this would hinder the child in the future instead of helping. Obviously, most parents are guilty of tyranny from time to time. Human motives are always mixed; and one does not always have time to think through one's commands fully, so that they will not always be fully appropriate. Yet the ideal of parenthood is that the parent will exercise authority, not tyranny. And the same is true of the use of power at every level of human authority.

To borrow more biblical language, authority is for "building up," not "tearing down." But even though those two activities seem to be diametrically opposed to one another, it is perilously easy for the powers of this world to slip from one into the other. If the English-speaking peoples have been relatively free of governmental tyranny over the last couple of centuries, that would not be true of our whole history—nor of the history of humanity as a whole. If Christianity itself was meant to act as an authority for human life, it, too, has often fallen into tyranny. The Jonestown debacle was an example of the way in which apparently good intentions may be perverted by a lack of realism in their execution. History offers many others, from the proverbial crimes of the Inquisition to the ongoing atrocities of religious conflict in Ireland or Lebanon or Bosnia.

We must, then, ask two questions about the Bible as authority: Does it fulfill the functions of an authority, as we have outlined them? And does it do so with realism, so that it does not fall into tyranny? The answer to both questions, I think, is "Yes," but we must survey these matters more closely.

A Sense of Identity and Hope

In what way does Scripture serve to give identity and hope? It gives us identity by showing us something of our beginning, and hope by showing us something of our end; for our beginning and our end alike are with God. Just as the child originates within the family and acquires a sense of identity from that origin, we, as human beings, have our origin with God. And, as members of the called people, in yet another sense, we have our origin from God. The Bible begins, quite rightly, with the creation, not as a scientific statement but as a statement about relationships. Genesis 1:26-27 tells us that we are all, male and female alike, made in the image and likeness of God. Genesis 2 contains a different narrative in which the very breath of humanity is the breath of God, by which God gave life to the first human being, Adam. All human beings, then, have a divine origin; all are presented (correctly, even from the point of view of modern biology) as being related to one another. We have, then, a relationship to God, like it or not, as certain as our relationship with each other. And we shall never know who we are or accept our identity until we have acknowledged that origin.

As Christians, however, we have still another kind of relationship with God, which further defines our identity: we are part of a called people. This special calling begins in Genesis 12, where God says to Abram, "Go from your country and your kindred and your father's house to the land that I will show you. I will make of you a great nation, and I will bless you, and make your name great, so that you will be a blessing" (vv. 1-2). In his subsequent dealings with Abram and his son and grandson, God refined this promise until at length there flowered from it the nation of Israel, the chosen people. To be a part of Israel was and is to be in a special relationship with God, founded not only on creation but also on the special call by which God sought their human cooperation.

Most Christians, however, being Gentiles by descent, cannot base their identity only on the call of Israel. Instead, we must look to a later calling, by which God brought about the existence of the church. Here, Gentiles, too, might become part of a chosen people and enjoy their own unique relationship with God—a relationship open to Israelites, as well, and on an equal footing. "Now in Christ Jesus you [Gentiles] who once were far off have been brought near by the blood of Christ" (Eph. 2:13). "Once you were not a people, but now you are God's people; once you had not received mercy, but now you have received mercy" (1 Pet. 2:10). Both as created and as called, we owe what we are to the initiatives of God.

It is this double identity, above all, which gives us a sense of hope for the future. If we are who we are as a result of what God has done, shall we not rely on God also to bring our lives and works to fruition? The whole course of creation from beginning to end is in God's hand—and we with it. At the end of the Bible, St. John gives this description of the life which is the goal of humanity: "I saw no temple in the city, for its temple is the Lord God the Almighty and the Lamb. And the city has no need of sun or moon to shine on it, for the glory of God is its light, and its lamp is the Lamb" (Rev. 21:22-23). Here is described for us a perfect intimacy with God, in which we are delivered from all unclarity and uncertainty, even with regard to ourselves.

Scripture, then, does indeed provide for those who read it both the foundation for their sense of identity and the grounds for their hope in the future. Because we have issued from the hand of God, we shall belong in the heavenly Jerusalem whose Temple God is. We shall rejoice to be there because it is our true home. It is not always easy to believe or to understand this. We are exceedingly complex creatures, after all, and hard to get to know. It is not at all surprising if we often doubt who we are. Yet we have an identity, for the almighty Maker has given us each the makings of it, so that we may proceed in hope.

Norms for Belief and Behavior

With this identity and this hope, of course, must also go some norms. In this respect, the Bible provides an embarrassment of riches—quite literally so, as we shall see. From the beginning of creation, according to Genesis 1, God gave certain rules of behavior: "Be fruitful and multiply, and fill the earth and subdue it; and have dominion over the fish" and other animals (Gen. 1:28). God also commanded (1:29f.) that human beings should eat a vegetarian diet and, by implication, that they were not to eat meat. Like the creation, the call of the chosen people is also associated with the giving of norms. In Genesis 12, as we have seen, Abram was not only singled out and given a call; he was also told to leave his homeland. Later on, he was given the commandment of circumcision. When the covenant with Abraham was further realized at Mount Sinai, many norms were now attached to it—norms both of belief and of practice. These range from the solemn magnificence of "Hear, O Israel: The Lord is our God, the Lord alone. You shall love the Lord your God with all your heart, and with all your soul, and with all your might" (Deut. 6:4-5) to the obscure particularity of "You shall not boil a kid in its mother's milk" (Exod. 34:26).

With the Christian calling, too, go certain norms, sometimes phrased in opposition to those of the earlier calling. "You have heard that it was said, 'You shall not commit adultery.' But I say to you that everyone who looks at a woman with lust has already committed adultery with her in his heart" (Matt. 5:27-28). On the other hand, certain norms were explicitly taken over from the older calling, including the *Shema* ("Hear, O Israel,...") and the famous verse of Leviticus, "You shall love your neighbor as yourself" (Mark 12:28-31). In yet other areas, the early Christians had to devise their own rules, as in the case of mixed marriages between Christians and pagans, where Paul tells us that he had no word of Jesus to guide him (1 Cor. 7:12f.).

Checking Our Performance

In the same way, the Bible offers many examples of the exercise of authority as a check on the individual's conformity to the norms. Sometimes these take on very dramatic forms, as in the story of David and Bathsheba. David the king had committed adultery with the beautiful Bathsheba and then sent her husband to certain death and taken her for his own wife. The prophet Nathan came to him afterwards and told him a story about a rich man who had taken his poor neighbor's pet lamb and served it to guests because he was too stingy to part with one of his own numerous animals. David, in a rage, said that the man deserved to die. Nathan replied, "You are the man" (2 Sam. 12:7). In a compelling way, David suddenly saw the full extent of his crime. He could say nothing other than "I have sinned against the Lord."

Other incidents may be less dramatic, but again and again throughout the Bible, notice is served on us that the called people do not live up to their calling. Joshua is represented as having predicted the failure of the chosen people: "You cannot serve the Lord, for he is a holy God. He is a jealous God; he will not forgive your transgressions or your sins" (Josh. 24:19). The prophets repeatedly charged the people with dereliction of the law: "They sell the righteous for silver, and the needy for a pair of sandals" (Amos 2:6). It might even be necessary for one inspired person to check the failures of another, as when Paul had his famous encounter with Peter: "When Cephas [that is, Peter] came to Antioch, I opposed him to his face, because he stood self-condemned; for until certain people came from James, he used to eat with the Gentiles. But after they came, he drew back and kept himself separate" (Gal. 2:11-12).

Jesus even sets up norms that are checks at the same time, for they are true norms (that is, true to our human condition, demanding of us things we can acknowledge as legitimate demands), and yet they are incapable of fulfillment (so that we are put perpetually on notice that we fall short). Consider such examples as these:

You have heard that it was said to those of ancient times, "You shall not murder"; and "whoever murders shall be liable to judgment." But I say to you that if you are angry with a brother or sister, you will be liable to judgment; and if you insult a brother or sister, you will be liable to the council; and if you say, "You fool," you will be liable to the hell of fire. (Matt. 5:21-22)

If your right eye causes you to sin, tear it out and throw it away; it is better for you to lose one of your members than for your whole body to be thrown into hell. (Matt 5:29)

Be perfect, therefore, as your heavenly Father is perfect. (Matt. 5:48)

These norms demand a degree of love, wholeness, and completeness that is appropriate to a humanity whose true home is in the heavenly city. Yet they are beyond our present capacity to achieve; indeed, to fulfill the commandment about the eye in any literal way could not possibly be right. Thus, we are reminded that we fall very short of the perfection that is our goal. In all these ways, then, the Bible provides the things we ask of authority: identity and hope, norms of belief and action, checks on one's achievement of those norms.

Biblical Authority
Or Biblical Tyranny?

There remains, however, the question whether the Scriptures do this with realism—or, to put it in other words, whether the Scriptures are authoritative for us or tyrannical. There can be no doubt that many people, particularly in our modern era, have seen them as the latter. They think of the Scriptures as setting up against human freedom a barricade of arbitrary "Thou shalt nots," or they think of the Bible as a tool in the hands of violent puritans who want to control society for their own narrow ends. How shall we deal with such accusations?

To begin with, we must admit that, on the historical level, they are true. The Bible has played a role in many tyrannies throughout the history of Christendom; it has often been a tool of repression, and it is still being used in that way by some. The theorists of slavery and racism, for example, used the Bible to justify the oppression of African-Americans in the U.S., and it appears that some South African Christians have done the same in recent times. The Bible, then, has been used to support various tyrannies, under various historical circumstances. We must even admit that the Bible actually contains elements tolerant of slavery, as we saw in the previous chapter.

I have already observed that the distance between the exercise of authority and that of tyranny is a short one in human experience. The fact that the Bible has sometimes been used in support of tyranny should not make us conclude automatically that it is a tyrannical book in and of itself. Indeed, there is one important element in Scripture that makes it impossible for the Bible to be such: a very large dose of ordinary, though well-polished, human wisdom.

To explain what I mean here, I must go back to my earlier example of parental authority. When a parent tells a child that she must do thus and so, it may be impossible to explain to the child why this is necessary. Yet even if that is impossible just now, the parent assumes that if the child could see the matter from the perspective of greater experience, the child would agree with the parent's judgment. There are dangers that only an adult can understand, yet the child would agree in wishing not to be maimed or killed, if she only understood that that danger was indeed present. Thus, we may say that authority, unlike tyranny, is capable of commanding the informed consent of the subject; if we truly understood our situation, we should agree with the command issued by the authority. A good parent works toward understanding.

What does this have to do with our relationship to God in Scripture? If God is truly God, that means that God is in a position analogous to that of the parent with the very young child: knowing immeasurably more about the world—and even about ourselves, in some ways—than we do. This means that we cannot rely on all of God's commands making immediate sense to us. Yet God in Scripture does not merely issue commands without explanation or justification. True, there are such commands in Scripture, but Scripture as a whole is not merely command. There is also a large element of human rationality in Scripture which makes an effort to interpret God's Word in terms that make sense in relation to what we know of life. Just as a parent may shout "Stop it!" at the child, but will also explain, "You will get hurt doing that," so also Scripture contains not only commands but also human efforts to understand the commands in terms of one's own experience.

There are whole books of Scripture, such as Proverbs, that are the distillation of the human wisdom of their day. Such works do not profess to be the voice of God speaking, but rather the voice of the wise. "The king's heart is a stream of water in the hand of the Lord; he turns it wherever he will" (Prov. 21:1). Is this a deep religious truth? No, it is a way of saying that one must not rely on the wielders of power, for their affection is as unpredictable as summer storms. In the same way, the author admonishes readers not to be enticed by the luxury of court life: "When you sit down to eat with a ruler, observe carefully what is before you, and put a knife to your throat if you have a big appetite" (Prov. 23:1-2).

Proverbs (and other Wisdom literature in the Old Testament) is full of such practical advice for the aspiring youth of antiquity, most of it having very little "religious" content.

The presence of such matter in Scripture amounts to an admission that there is, after all, some value in human wisdom. We are not mere sticks and stones to be shifted around at will by some higher power. We, too, possess some understanding of life, and the Bible acknowledges that this human understanding must be brought into play. I don't mean to suggest that every command in the Bible or every claim to belief is somehow made clear in terms of this human wisdom; that is not the case. I only mean to point out that the Bible as a whole recognizes the importance of our rationality.

This fact in itself refutes anyone who might wish to take some set of biblical commandments and impose them on the world without any effort to make sense of them in terms we can understand. The Bible, taken as a whole, is not that kind of book. Granted that human understanding is incomplete and that we must always take a good deal "on faith" (whether faith in the Christian Gospel or in something else), it remains true that our faith should ultimately be intelligible. That means that it should at least begin to make sense in terms of the reality we know here and now.

Authority for Today---- Or a History of Authority?

I have argued, thus far, that the Bible fits our basic conception of what authority is. It provides identity and hope, a set (in fact, several sets) of norms, and checks on how we measure up to them. All this it does with a certain realism, exemplified in the Bible's inclusion of much purely human wisdom. There remains, however, a major problem in all this. I have said that the Bible "provides" all this, but I might better have said that it "provided" it. For the Scriptures are not addressed directly to us, as if to provide us all these things here and now. Instead, the Scriptures are made up of a variety of books originally addressed to other people at many different times and places. The result is a certain confusion, in that Scripture offers us *not one* identity (and so forth) *but many,* coupled with a certain distance in that all these were offered originally to someone else.

The Bible, to put it another way, is rather like a historical record of the exercise of authority; it does not simply express authority for us in our own circumstances. Consider, for example, the issue of identity. We have noted that the Gospel offers a relationship with God that is open to both Israel and the Gentiles. What, then, are we to do with that earlier relationship which God contracted particularly with Abraham and his descendants? Some Christians have supposed that the church has taken the place of Israel as God's called people, but we can scarcely accept that. If God can retract his promise to Israel, how can we rely on his promised relationship with us? Of course, this is no new problem; New Testament writers such as Paul were already struggling with it. He concluded that the essential characteristic of Abraham was *faith* and that all who shared his faith could also share the special relationship granted to him and his descendants (Romans 4).

It is clear that there has been a change in point of view between the Law of Moses and the Gospel preached by Paul. Paul himself, in fact, insists on it. This means that the whole issue of identity, for Paul, is posed in terms different from those of the Law: "If it is the adherents of the law who are to be the heirs, faith is null and the promise is void" (Rom. 4:14). But if authority is now redefining our identity, it must also redefine the norms that go along with it—just as we have seen Jesus doing. This means that the Bible is full of norms which most Christians regard as inactive for them. The result is that one cannot simply go to the Bible unaided and pick out which commands are in force and which are not.

Take, for example, the Ten Commandments (Exod. 20:1-17). One often sees them posted in Christian churches or hears them read or invoked as authoritative. Yet there is one among the ten which the vast majority of Christians break quite routinely and with no sense of guilt: "Remember the sabbath day, and keep it holy....you shall not do any work" (vv. 8, 10). Some Christians do observe this commandment in a way, by applying it to Sunday—though I think few Christians are really strict about this any more. But the commandment does not refer to Sunday at all. The word "sabbath" means the period from sunset on Friday to sunset on Saturday. It is a Hebrew word with a quite specific meaning, and it cannot be forced to mean something else. There are a few modern Christian sects that recognize this, and rather than break one of the Ten Commandments, they have insisted that their members not work on Saturdays. From the earliest times, however, the great majority of Christians (following Jesus' own example) ceased to regard this commandment as binding. The average American Christian of today who mows the lawn or goes to the grocery on Saturday is certainly not conscious of violating God's expressed will.

What is true of our identity and of the biblical norms is even more true of the checks in Scripture. Nathan could stand before David to call his sin to his consciousness; he does not stand before us to appraise our own individual situations. There are times, to be sure, when a word of Scripture speaks to us so piercingly that we cannot avoid seeing ourselves in a new light. But the written word can never offer the individual checks that a living person can; it cannot stand beside us like a teacher and say, "Here you have it right, and there you have it wrong."

In sum, it appears that the Bible is not a complete authority, after all. It does all the things that we expect an authority to do, but it does not do them effectively by itself. Perhaps Paul does resolve the most crucial question for us—the question of identity. We as Gentiles can understand how to read the Old Testament and find God speaking to us in it, for Paul has shown us how we, too, may be children of Abraham and heirs of the promises made to him. But the question of norms is not settled anywhere in Scripture itself—not clearly, at least. Nowhere does a New Testament writer clearly abrogate the law of the sabbath for later Christians; at the same time, it is clear from other New Testament passages that the full law is no longer binding on all Christians. Paul, for example, successfully demonstrated in Galatians that it is not necessary for Gentile Christian males to be circumcised. How is one to pick and choose among the multitudinous commandments? How is one to know which are to be obeyed and which are not?

Most Christians never think twice about such questions unless they are confronted with the reality that different Christian communities themselves may differ in the matter. The same chapter that tells us not to work on Saturday also tells us not to commit murder. How does one know that the one commandment still avails and the other does not? The very same verse (Lev. 19:26) that forbids witchcraft also forbids eating meat that has not been slaughtered in a kosher way. How does the Christian "know" that the one commandment still holds and the other does not? Clearly, there is more to the question of authority than we have yet seen. The Bible, it seems, is not the only authority for Christians, no matter how much some may insist that it is. There are other authorities which work alongside it, ones we must now also consider.

Chapter 3

Authority for Christians

The Authority of the Creator

In a sense, there can be only one true authority—God alone. By the classical definition, Christians conceive of God as radically other than the creation. God alone is complete and sufficient, always able to give, not requiring any correction or support from another source. In comparison, every lesser authority is severely limited. We can be in only one place at one time, which limits our knowledge; our comprehension, too, is finite, so that we do not even understand everything that we experience. Any parent, for instance, must wonder occasionally whether authority has been used in the best way for his or her child. To some extent, even the best efforts made in raising our children prepare them only for life as we know it, since we cannot predict what the world will be like when they are adults.

In addition to these limits on our presence, knowledge, and understanding, we also experience the limits of our own good will. Human authorities, from parents to presidents, not only make mistakes and errors of judgment; they also at times turn into tyrants, exercising their power to gratify their own interests or whims and not to fulfill the needs of their subjects. At a very minimum, I imagine that every parent is conscious of having spoken sharply to a child out of his or her own frustrations at some time or other, rather than out of a justified concern about what the child was doing. At the maximum, history discloses instances of incredible crimes in church and state, committed to satisfy the egotism of one or a few people—such as the Inquisition and the Holocaust.

No created authority can be free of such things. Humanity as we know it is "fallen" and there is no reason to think that human authorities will ever be free of the danger of lapsing into tyranny. But even an unfallen humanity would, it seems, be liable to the other restrictions of existence in the created order—finitude and ignorance. Such an authority will inevitably, at times, give us misdirections, a false sense of identity and hope, wrong norms, mistaken checks.

God alone can announce our identity to us with absolute assurance, since God is the source of all things. God is the one who proclaims our true hope, being the lover of the creation and its end. God can issue true and unvarying norms because God is everywhere the same. When checking how we measure up to these norms, God is always in the right, as having unlimited knowledge. Moreover, no one more than God can guarantee the realism of authority, for only God is free of the evil will that urges us to tyranny. As the source of all things, God cannot fail to understand the course of the universe truly and provide for it faithfully. In God, all the failures and inadequacies that afflict human authorities are made good.

None of this is self-evident, of course. It is not inevitable that one believe in a God at all or suppose that there is any divine and personal order to this universe in which we live. Much less is it inevitable that one believe in a God who is all-powerful, all-knowing, all-wise, and fundamentally beneficent. If there are good things in our experience that make such a God credible, there are also the evils of suffering and death which make it difficult to believe in that same God. But this is a question that must be argued elsewhere and in other ways. My point here is that this kind of God is assumed in the Christian Gospel. Those who believe in such a God will need to recognize that in this God alone is authority fully realized, fully achieved, and beyond question. In the absolute sense, authority is God's alone.

Unfortunately, this authority is not directly accessible to us. The Bible contains the record of the many and various ways in which God has spoken to human beings: through dreams, visions, prophetic oracles, human wisdom, and angelic and human messengers. There is no reason to deny that God still speaks in these ways. But God speaks when and as God pleases. Often it is hard to be sure God has spoken, and the answer may not seem to correspond to our questions. The God of Israel holds no audiences where we may offer our petitions and secure a clear answer: Is abortion ever permissible? May homosexual persons be ordained to the ministry? What is the meaning of this or that text of Scripture? Even though God is the only absolute authority conceivable, we do not have useful access to God for our present purposes.

The Authority of Jesus

But has God not become available to us within the context of this world? Is this not the meaning of the Incarnation (the Word become flesh)—that Jesus embodies God within the framework of space and time? Already in the New Testament books, Christians had begun to speak of Jesus in such a way, and later Christian reflection has made it a standard of orthodoxy. His name is "Emmanuel," "God-with-us," and somehow the absoluteness of God is incorporated in him, to proclaim God's love, to declare God's will, to judge our obedience and our failure. The orthodox Christian teaching, founded on the New Testament, is that this Incarnation is eternal and that Jesus even now lives to carry on this mission. To his followers he said, "Remember, I am with you always, to the end of the age" (Matt. 28:20).

Whatever this promise may mean, however, it does not mean that Jesus is still with us in tangible, accessible form. He could not be. The Incarnation means that he is not only truly God but also truly human. No human being remains forever in this life; finiteness is a condition of our existence, without which we should not be truly human. As human beings—at least, in this part of our pilgrimage—we are bound to the world of change and becoming, growth and decay. And we must belong to a particular community in a particular place and time, speaking its language and contending with its verities. In all these ways, Jesus was truly human. Even though his presence is truly felt among Christians today in Word and Sacrament, his *person* is that of a man of Palestine in the first century of our era.

As such, Jesus spoke to people of his time—to Pharisees and Sadducees, to peasants and centurions, to priests, to prostitutes, and to a Roman governor. No doubt, we have things in common with all these people—pride, selfishness, fear, hope, love; but we *are* not any of them. Indeed, our world is radically different from theirs in many respects. Today, Judaism is more unified, and

Greco-Roman paganism has disappeared. The prevailing political philosophy is democracy or socialism, not monarchy. We live in an urban, industrial economy, not an agrarian one. One could make quite a long list, but the point should be clear enough. If we consider how much of our lives and behavior is dictated (or, at least, shaped) by our job, our family relationships, and the kind of community we live in, we shall easily see that a change of culture means a change in individuals, too. To take but one example, how would your life be different if, like most Greek and Roman householders, you had at least one slave living with you? How much more, if you were the slave?

We do not need to be nineteen and a half centuries away from Jesus to realize that he was bound to his own place and time. The earliest Christians already began to realize this and to see that they would need to supplement or revise some of his sayings in order to make Christianity work in other times and places. Jesus' audience was predominantly Jewish and Palestinian. When he spoke of marriage, he did so in terms of the institutions actually existing among his audience: "I say to you that anyone who divorces his wife, except on the ground of unchastity, causes her to commit adultery; and whoever marries a divorced woman commits adultery" (Matt. 5:32). In accordance with the Law of Moses, Jesus speaks only of the husband divorcing the wife, since the Law made no provision for women to divorce their husbands. But the Christian community did not long stay confined to Jewish Palestine; it spread quickly to the Gentile world, too. There, women could divorce their husbands, and Christians quickly transferred what Jesus had said about men to women as well: "To the married," says Paul, "I give this command—not I but the Lord—that the wife should not separate from her husband" (1 Cor. 7:10).

Yet this was not enough. Some situations were so new that there was no way simply to extend a saying of Jesus to cover them. In such cases, the early Christians were willing to supplement freely. After the passage quoted above, Paul went on to write, "To the rest I say—I and not the Lord—that if any believer has a wife who is an unbeliever, and she consents to live with him, he should not divorce her," and the same with the Christian woman married to an unbelieving husband. "But if the unbelieving partner separates, let it be so; in such a case the brother or sister is not bound" (1 Cor. 7:12-15). This was a situation that could scarcely have arisen during Jesus' own ministry; hence, he never addressed himself to it. Paul, however, was not at all embarrassed to go beyond what Jesus had said in order to provide direction for new situations.

Is Jesus, then, so bound to his original culture that he has nothing to say to us today? By no means. He speaks to us, through the record of Scripture, in two ways. He says some things to us when we see ourselves in continuity with the ancient people who formed his original audience. Much of the time, that is easy to do. Jesus told a story about the Pharisee and the tax collector who went up to the Temple to pray (Luke 18:10-14). The Pharisee prayed proudly, noting how much better he was than this tax collector. The tax collector, on the other hand, claimed nothing for himself but asked forgiveness for his sins. Jesus praised the tax collector for his prayer. It is not difficult to see something of each of these persons in ourselves, for we know our own pride and our own sin and our failure to control either one.

Again, Jesus speaks to us out of the past when he says certain things in such a way as to apply them universally. For example, he cited two commandments as summarizing the whole Law and Prophets: "You shall love the Lord your God with all your heart, and with all your soul, and with all your mind"; and "You shall love your neighbor as yourself" (Mark 12:28-31). This utterance is general enough to apply to all human situations, and it means as much for us today as for the people of Jesus' own time. Yet for just this reason, its usefulness is limited, for it is hard to take so general a commandment and apply it in specific situations. What does it mean, for example, in dealing with the terminally ill, to love God and to love my neighbor as myself? Jesus clarified the meaning of the commandments somewhat by telling the story of the Good Samaritan (Luke 10:29-37). He showed that we must not limit the term "neighbor" to those who are tied to us by kinship, affection, or mutual good will. But in the very nature of the case, no one can say in advance exactly what the commandment will mean in every possible situation.

However highly we regard Jesus, then, he is not the final solution to the problem of authority. Like God, he is less than fully accessible to us in our own time and place. He was and is God with us---but with us in the person of a particular human being of a certain place and time. Like every human being Jesus is bound to his point in history, and his message can transcend it only in part. He is no more present for the settling of our modern uncertainties than is his Father. For other purposes, indeed, both are fully present---for giving of life and strength and grace and hope. Not, however, for the easy settling of questions and conflicts.

The Authority of the Holy Spirit

There is yet another presence of God, however, that we have been promised. Perhaps this is the solution to our difficulty: "I still have many things to say to you [this is Jesus speaking to his disciples], but you cannot bear them now. When the Spirit of truth comes, he will guide you into all the truth" (John 16:12-13). From the beginning, Christians have believed this promise earnestly and expected that the Holy Spirit would direct and guide the church through spirit-filled people such as apostles and prophets. There has never been a time when Christians have abandoned this expectation. Sometimes Christians have expected these servants of the Spirit to be manifested through charismatic phenomena, such as miracles or speaking in tongues. At other times, most Christians have felt that such phenomena were incidental. Always, however, they have expected the Spirit to speak in their own day through inspired people, relying not just on human wisdom and knowledge to lead the church but contributing that insight and understanding which the Spirit alone can give.

Here, surely, is the solution to the problem of authority. For the Spirit is accessible through inspired people and is equally close to us in every age, being bound to no one time or place. Yet here, too, we find ourselves in difficulty, for the various people who lay claim to speak for the Spirit do not always agree, and we have no sure way of telling which of them might have the more authentic voice. This problem was already afflicting the earliest Christians, as we can see from the New Testament. Peter and Paul were both spirit-filled people; and yet we have already made note of the collision between them at Antioch, as recorded by Paul in Galatians 2. How should we have known, under the circumstances, which to follow?

The early Christians also found that some people who claimed to be speaking under the inspiration of the Spirit were really uttering things contrary to the Gospel; and they deduced from this that not every spirit-filled person was speaking by *the* Spirit. They believed that there were many spirits abroad in the world and that any of them might take possession of a person. Hence, the Christian community had to learn how to distinguish true spirits from false. The First Epistle of John offers one such test:

> Beloved, do not believe every spirit, but test the spirits to see whether they are from God; for many false prophets have gone out into the world. By this you know the Spirit of God: every spirit that confesses that Jesus Christ has come in the flesh is from God, and every spirit that does not confess Jesus is not from God. (1 John 4:1-3)

At a slightly later date, we have rules for distinguishing true prophets from false in the early Christian writing called the Teaching of the Twelve Apostles *(Didache)*. For example, a true prophet, under inspiration, may order a banquet to be served up; but if he eats of it himself, he is just trading on Christ *(Didache* 11.9).

Even these rules, however, are not much help, for they were designed to meet problems of their own day. The author of 1 John was probably combatting an early Christian heresy called Docetism, which taught that Jesus did not have a real, material body and therefore did not suffer on the cross. In sum, he only *seemed* or *appeared* to have been human. Like many other Christian leaders, this writer felt that such a teaching was contrary to the Gospel and deprived the Christian message of its power. He could not accept the idea that any true, prophetic spirit would utter such an idea. But what of later controversies, such as those over the Trinity? Did it follow, from what John wrote, that so long as a prophet was willing to admit that Jesus had come in the flesh, it made no difference whether he was willing to confess one God in three persons? Not at all. As new issues arose, new ways of "testing" the spirits had to be formulated. As for the Teaching of the Twelve Apostles *(Didache),* its rules were formulated in terms of first-century village life, and some would be hard to apply in a twentieth-century city.

In our own day, no one can fail to be aware that there are many different varieties of Christianity in circulation. Each claims to represent the will of God. Some claim exclusive possession of God's good will, while others are willing to claim only that they share in it; yet there is surely no Christian community that does not believe it represents what the Spirit wishes to say to people in our world. In some cases, the disagreement among Christians is quite serious, and it seems scarcely possible that all sides could be right. And yet, we do not have incontestable rules today for testing the spirits. The result is that the Spirit, like the Father and the Son, turns out to be inaccessible as our authority. The Spirit is fully accessible to us in a host of other respects—in prayer, in love, in the communion of holy things and people; but God, it seems, does not intend to be directly accessible to us as authority.

Scripture Is Not God

It is no surprise, then, that many Christians over the ages have turned to the Bible to make up for the lack of absolute authority in this world. The transition, it seems, is fairly easy. Is not the Bible the Word of God? Then does it not somehow bring down into our uncertain existence the absolute certainty and security of God's life? No, it does not. We have already seen, just by looking carefully at Scripture, that it does not have the kind of infallibility that we ascribe to God. We must now go on to see why that should be so—indeed, must be so.

I have already observed that everything in this creation is bound to particular places and times. Even in the case of the Incarnation, God the Son became in Jesus a particular human being in a particular place and time. He spoke to the people of that place and time in terms familiar to them from their own culture. His knowledge, like that of any human being (for he was truly human), was limited by the knowledge possible for an individual of that culture. I don't mean that he was merely an ordinary person-in-the-street. No, he possessed extraordinary and unique insight into the purposes of God. But he was not, as a human being, all-knowing. He himself confessed that he did not know exactly when the end of the world would take place (Mark 13:32). And I think it safe to say that if you could have asked him a question about quantum physics, you would have met with a blank look, for the term did not even exist in the world of his day.

What was true of the Incarnate God must also be true—even more so—of the Bible. Is the Bible itself God? No Christian would dare to say that. It is rather the Word of God, one great way which God has of addressing us within the confines of this created universe. That means that the Scriptures as we have them are an artifact of this world, the work of human minds and lips and hands, under the inspiration of God. If they were perfect in every respect, they would no longer belong to this world at all. The first copy of the Ten Commandments, we are told, was written by the finger of God himself. But Moses smashed this copy when he came down from the mountain and saw the golden calf (Exod. 32:15-19), for such holiness could find no place among the sinful people. The second copy, long preserved in the Ark of the Covenant, seems to have been the work of Moses himself (Exod. 34:28). This is a kind of parable of the whole of Scripture. The Word of God can be brought to humanity only by the agency of some creature, speaking in a language we understand. In the process, some element of creatureliness cannot but enter into the final product. The Bible, then, cannot be absolute as God is; for then it would *be* God. And like God in all other respects, it would be inaccessible to us in our need, standing beyond the confines of this world.

What, then, remains? God, who is the absolute authority for Christians, remains largely inaccessible to us for this purpose. When God does become accessible, through the creation or the Incarnation of the Son or the inspiration of the Spirit, or through God's Word in Scripture, divine authority is qualified by the very fact that it is brought down into this world and conditioned by the limitations of time and place. Does this mean that we are all cast loose from our moorings and left with no source of authority in which we can trust? In one sense, yes. There is no absolute authority at all within the confines of this created universe. The world to come, in which we are to enjoy the immediate presence of God in some new way, seems to promise a nearer approach to such absolute authority, but it does not offer itself to us here and now. In another sense, however, we are not at all lacking in authority for our existence in this world; but the authority we have is of the kind appropriate for us—an authority existing in the same time and space as we ourselves do, and limited by that fact.

Practical Authority:
The Christian Community

The authority of which I speak is the authority on which all Christians rely most of the time: the authority of the Christian community to which they belong. I am speaking, for now, in terms of what actually happens in our experience. Why is it that an Episcopalian feels no guilt about working on the sabbath, while a Seventh-Day Adventist does? Scripture itself does not explicitly settle the matter, despite some claims on both sides. Yet neither person is apt to feel any difficulty in the matter. Why do some people grow up assuming that the Bible prohibits the use of alcohol, while others grow up assuming that it permits it? Why do some Christians feel that the Lord's Supper has been duly celebrated only when an ordained person presides at the table, while others feel that they have been truer to Jesus' memory when a lay person presides? In all these matters and many more, it is the Christian community to which the believer belongs that makes the decision. No doubt a reverence for the Bible entered into the original making of the decision, and no doubt the church will claim biblical warrant for its practice and teaching. But if all churches are equally right at all points in making this claim, it seems to imply that the Bible gives a multifarious set of directions.

Some, of course, will seek to cut this Gordian knot by claiming that their church is correct and truly biblical, while all others are more or less mistaken. One should reflect, however, on the implications of such a claim and consider whether they are believable. Such a claim requires us to believe, no matter what church we adhere to, that there are vast masses of thoughtful, educated, and devout Christian people in the world who have entirely missed the point of Scripture. Why? How could such a thing happen? Are all these people less devout or less serious about the Word of God than the people of my own church? That will be very difficult to demonstrate, and the more one comes to know Christians of other persuasions, the more difficult one finds it to maintain. Are they, then, simply ignorant or imperceptive? The chances are that in any large group of human beings, the distribution of intelligence will be pretty much the same. Education, of course, is another matter, but every major Christian tradition has its scholars who have undertaken some kind of serious study of Scripture. We cannot, then, attribute all the differences among churches either to lack of devotion or to lack of understanding.

The Scriptures, it seems, really are open to a variety of interpretations. I do not mean to say that one can get anything at all out of the Bible. Christians today, as in the past, are agreed on certain matters: the centrality of Jesus in God's purpose for humanity, the identity of the God of Jesus with the Creator of the world, and so forth. But within the broad limits of basic and inescapable Christian belief, the Bible allows much room for variation.

As human beings, however, we can live with only so much uncertainty. I cannot decide anew every Saturday whether Scripture allows me to mow the lawn or forbids it. I cannot return to all the relevant texts of Scripture and analyze them theologically all over again each week, to find out what the Word of God seems to be saying this time. Indeed, if my life has not allowed me to enter into a deep and detailed study of the Bible, I may not even know where to find all the relevant passages, or how to deal with them once found. We require ready-made answers to a great many questions, even if they are not always perfect answers.

The Christian communities to which we belong, then, serve an indispensable function. They are our *practical* authorities, from which we acquire the identity and hope, the norms and the checks, that make daily life possible within a meaningful framework. Unlike God, they are very far from being absolute authorities, but also unlike God, they are accessible here and now to fulfill our needs.

Does this mean that we can dispense with the Bible altogether? There have been times when Christians have functioned as if that were possible. Some Christian communities have subordinated the Bible almost entirely to the community's traditional interpretation of it. This was largely true of Roman Catholicism before the Second Vatican Council; it is true, at the other end of the spectrum, of contemporary American Fundamentalism. The assumption has been that everything important the Bible had to say is already known to the community and that the Bible itself need be used only to prove this fact. I hope to show, however, that this is a misunderstanding of the relationship between the Bible and the Christian community.

At this point, I simply want to make it clear that the Christian community always has been and must always be the practical authority for Christian life in this world.

How else could it be? In a world determined by space and time, authority must be authority for us, here and now, in concrete and accessible ways. The utterances of authority in one century will not always work as planned in another. Even the American Constitution could scarcely function under our changed circumstances if it had not been reinterpreted to meet new situations. And we have already seen that early Christians found it necessary to do the same with the words of Jesus. In order for authority to be authority for our time and place, it must lie in the hands of contemporary people and communities, who can speak to a situation that no earlier authority could have fully foreseen.

Different Christian communities, of course, have embodied this authority in different ways. One community may embody it in a hierarchical structure in which only a few persons have the privilege and duty of uttering authoritative pronouncements. Another may have a democratic constitution which leaves the authority primarily in the hands of the assembled people. One community may express its norms through written statements and yet be willing to tolerate a good deal of variance from them, while another leaves its norms largely unexpressed but is prepared to expel all violators immediately. For our present purposes, it makes little difference how each Christian community embodies authority. It is enough to recognize that all the faithful rely on their communities for this purpose.

Community of Faith and Individual Believer

It may seem to some, however, that I am stressing the role of the community too much, at the expense of the individual. It has been an axiom of Protestantism in general and of American Protestantism in particular that the individual believer can appeal from the authority of the community to that of the Bible. If the individual, like Luther, can show that the church has ignored some great truth of Scripture, we feel that rebellion against the church's tradition is justified. This is an axiom with which I am in full agreement. Details of the relationship between church and Scripture will be addressed in the next chapter, but it is important to say something here about the individual and the church.

We all know that the individual may come into conflict with the church, for it has happened repeatedly in the last few centuries of church history, sometimes in spectacular and dramatic ways. It would be a mistake, though, to focus exclusively on the possibility of opposition between the two without seeing that individual and community are also closely linked in two important ways. First of all, the individual who turns to the reading of the Bible is not a tabula rasa. We all go to Scripture with certain preformed notions about what is true and what is false, what is Christian and what is not. If we have Christian backgrounds, our expectations of the Bible will represent largely those of the community in which we have received our impressions of Christianity. Quite likely, we do not agree with our community in every detail, but we have absorbed its overall faith and cannot avoid reading the Bible in terms of it. Thus, the individual who reads Scripture is a product of the community.

Secondly, however, we must remember that the individual believer is also a contributor to the Christian community. No community is invulnerable to change, though some do resist it. All life involves both change and continuity; objects, such as mountains, which seem never to change in our experience of them, we do not think of as alive. A living community, then, will change, whether it is conscious of it or not. The source of these changes, typically, will be individual members of the community—individuals who have begun to see some altered vision of their faith that meets new circumstances. Thus, Luther may have begun as one who challenged his community, but he ended as one who reshaped it radically. The ongoing exchange between the individual believer and the community's tradition is the means of the church's life.

The authority of the Christian community, then, is not a monolithic power nor is it a dead hand from the past. Even the most hierarchical churches are responsive, over a period of time, to the changing perspectives of their members. All churches find it necessary to make new decisions about how they will meet new needs, and all churches have been known to change their minds at times, even if they do not advertise the fact.

It remains true, however, that our communities give us the provisional authority for living in the present. For this purpose, churches do not have to be infallible—and I know of no church that explicitly claims to be. (Roman Catholic claims about the infallibility of the papacy amount to less than that, I think.) Nor if we look back over the history of Christianity with some detachment can we easily believe in an infallible church. What we ask of the church, however, is only provisional. To be a Methodist, a Baptist, or a Roman Catholic—is this the same identity we shall have when we become citizens of the heavenly Jerusalem? Hardly. To be a Christian by whatever name is an identity of this world, ultimately to be dissolved into the more perfect identity of the redeemed in the world to come.

In sum, then, the church is our immediate and practical authority, standing under the final authority of God. Where does the Bible fit into this picture? It is neither God nor church; yet Christians will agree, I think, that it holds its own indispensable place in the whole structure of authority for Christian life. In the next chapter, we will try to understand what that place is.

Chapter 4

Scripture and the Church

The history of the relationship between the Bible and the church is a mixed one and shows that the two are interdependent. Each is dependent on the other for its existence; each is, in some sense, subject to the other's judgment. To begin with, let us explore the dependence of the Bible on the church, for here we are dealing with simple, historical facts, easy enough to describe and analyze. The Scriptures are dependent on the community of faith (first Israel, later the church as well) for their very existence, in two senses: the writings arose out of the life of the community, and the community then defined the *canon* or authoritative list of those books it considered to be Sacred Scripture. It is thus legitimate to speak of the community of faith, under God, as having created the Scriptures.

Scripture as the Church's Book

Consider the books of the *New Testament*. They were written by Christian authors for a Christian audience; some of them were even called forth by the immediate needs of specific Christian congregations. Paul's First Letter to the Corinthians, for example, is hardly intelligible without reference to the life of the quarrelsome and unruly congregation to which he wrote. In it, he discussed many matters of enduring interest to believers— for example, the unity of the church, sexual ethics, the Lord's Supper, gifts of the Spirit, and the resurrection. Yet he chose these topics not because of their enduring significance but because they were occasions of trouble and dissent in the congregation at Corinth. In a somewhat different vein, the Revelation to John was written to meet the needs of Christians about to undergo persecution. It tries to supply an encouraging overview of their specific situation, with the guarantee that God is still in control no matter how bad things may get.

Even the Gospels and the Acts of the Apostles met certain needs within the earliest Christian communities. They helped to preserve the record of Jesus' deeds and words in a time when the eyewitnesses were dying or memory was fading. They presented these accounts in ways that would be useful in directing church life or in refuting certain heresies. Matthew's Gospel has been called a "manual" of church life, and while that is an exaggeration, the author did indeed arrange the teachings of Jesus into a series of coherent, useful discourses (for example, the Sermon on the Mount). John's Gospel, on the other hand, has elements that show that its author wanted to emphasize the reality of Jesus' body as against the contemporary Docetist heretics. The Gospel of Luke and its sequel, the Acts of the Apostles, offer a great deal of legal material, which the early Christians may have used to try to persuade Roman officials that there was no official Roman policy against Christianity. In short, the

New Testament writers did not write only from some creative urge but because they saw that their writings would be useful in the context of the life of the church.

This does not contradict the idea that the Spirit inspired these writers. Rather, it tells something about the way in which the Spirit worked with them. The authors did not work as isolated individuals with the Spirit as their only company, perched on their shoulders in the form of a dove and whispering Greek into their ears. John, to be sure, was a lonely exile when he wrote the Revelation, but the contents of his work make it clear that his heart and mind were with the faithful he had left behind in the province of Asia. All of our writers were conscious of the roles they were playing in the Christian community. The Spirit did not short-circuit the normal process of composition in their case, but filled and informed it.

Just as the New Testament books arose out of the life of the church, so also the books of the *Old Testament* (or the Hebrew Bible) arose out of the life of the church's parent or elder sibling, the people of Israel. The Law of Moses was their constitution, and the books of history were their history. The prophets arose from time to time in order to intervene in their public life, recalling them to faithfulness in their God and rebuking the oppressors of the poor. The Wisdom writers both recorded the traditional wisdom of the Israelite schools and pondered on the theological problems of their own times. All their writings were the work of people involved in a community and making a contribution to its life.

Both Israel and the church, however, produced many books other than the few that eventually became the Bible. The *canon* (or official list of scriptural books) that we acknowledge represents a selection made by the community of faith from among the available titles. The church, of course, derived its Old Testament from the Scriptures of Israel, but not in final form. The New Testament reveals some disagreement as to the exact contents of the Old, for the Epistle of Jude cites material from two books, 1 Enoch and the Assumption of Moses, which you will not find in English translations of the Bible. (Only the Ethopian Church regards 1 Enoch as Scripture; the Assumption of Moses is not in any church's canon.)

To this day, there are disagreements among Christians about the exact extent of the Old Testament canon. The early Greek-speaking Christians took over the Greek version of the Jewish Scriptures, the Septuagint, for their Old Testament. But a number of books in the Septuagint were not included in the Hebrew-Aramaic canon as it was eventually shaped by the rabbis. Indeed, different copies of the Septuagint itself might contain slightly different lists of books. Thus it came about that a number of books, such as 4 Maccabees and the Wisdom of Solomon, have remained in an uncertain position. The Eastern Orthodox alone accept 4 Maccabees; they and the Roman Catholics accept the Wisdom of Solomon; Protestants will at most concede that the books may be included in a secondary collection called the Apocrypha of the Old Testament. Yet the Protestant Apocrypha includes one book, 2 Esdras, which has no canonical status for the Eastern Orthodox or the Roman Catholics. It is a confusing situation, for which there is no easy resolution.

The early Christians, then, agreed that there was such a thing as Scripture; but from the earliest days, there was some disagreement as to the exact canon. Israel itself had not yet come to agreement on the question, and the

Christians used whatever books they inherited without being too precise about the matter. There was as yet no New Testament, of course, for the books that form our New Testament were produced only gradually through the first and early second centuries; and they were not considered scriptural in the beginning. Over the decades of the early second century, however, Christians began to read certain of their own writings, particularly the Gospels, in church alongside the Scriptures of Israel. It was this use of the Christian writings in worship which led the church to create a New Testament. Yet the contents of this specifically Christian canon were as uncertain at first as the contents of the Old Testament.

There was no central authority in the church of the early Roman Empire that could settle the matter. Instead, each important local church had its own list of books approved for reading in church. Some books acquired a very wide acceptance from an early time. Thus, the four Gospels were generally acknowledged by the late second century—though even then some questioned the Gospel of John, perhaps because it was so different from the other three. Also, certain of the Pauline letters were widely accepted, though there was some uncertainty about the pastoral epistles (1 and 2 Timothy and Titus). The Acts of the Apostles was accepted along with Luke's Gospel, but the remaining books of the New Testament only gained full approval gradually, particularly 2 Peter and the Revelation to John. Not only was the church hesitant to accept some books that belong to our modern New Testament, but it also considered including a few that were ultimately disallowed. The Shepherd of Hermas was regarded as scriptural by some, as were the Epistle of Barnabas and the Apocalypse of Peter. Some New Testament manuscripts from as late as the fourth century include the Teaching of the Twelve Apostles *(Didache)* or the two letters of Clement.

How was all this uncertainty resolved? By a *gradual process* of comparison and adjustment among different Christian congregations. There was never a council that settled the issue, nor some individual hierarch whose word carried the weight of law. People sometimes date the completed canon to the Easter Letter of A.D. 367, in which St. Athanasius, patriarch of Alexandria, listed the New Testament books that were binding for Egypt. It is indeed the first list that is identical with our modern canon, but it did not settle the issue. The church did not create the canon of Scripture by decree but through the gradual consensus of Christian people.

Yet the Bible is not simply the creation of the church. The churches accepted these particular books at least in part because of the profound impression the books made on the Christian people. It would be hard to account for the presence of Philemon or Jude or 3 John in this way; they were included more for the sake of the prestigious names attached to them. For the most part, however, the churches were giving testimony to what they perceived as the quality of the books themselves. The development of the canon was thus a two-way street: certain books made a profound impression on the churches, which, in turn, set them apart as enjoying a particularly sacred and authoritative status.

The Church as Interpreter of Scripture

The dependence of the Bible on the church did not end with the formulation of the canon. Even as the Christian

Bible was being assembled and set apart, people were encountering the problem of interpretation. Both the passage of time and the selection of the canon made this inevitable. The Scriptures do not interpret themselves; if they did, we should not have as many disagreements among Christians as we do. The Bible contains no one ready-made system for resolving the differences and conflicts that it contains, nor does it tell us how to translate its message into terms that will make sense in our own very different historical and cultural context. Already in the Israel of Jesus' time, the problem of interpretation had become acute; it was a major point of contention between Sadducees, Pharisees, and other Jewish religious leaders. The need was certainly no less for the church, which had come to believe that the real point of all Scripture was to be found in the life, death, and resurrection of Jesus.

The church has labored at the task of interpreting Scripture over a long time and in a variety of ways. There have been some Christian communities in which the interpretation of Scripture is the business only of the hierarchy or of ordained persons. Other communities have insisted on the active involvement of the lay people. Some Christians have stressed the importance of education as a preparation for interpreting the Bible, while others have felt that the novice interpreter might do better than the educated one, provided the Spirit directs his or her work. The churches, then, have done the work of interpretation through a variety of personnel.

Literal-Allegorical Interpretation

The churches have also embraced an astonishing variety of methods in interpreting the Bible. The history of biblical interpretation is a fascinating and thought-provoking field, since it shows that, however constant Christians have been in their reverence for the Bible, they have sometimes invoked radically different methods for understanding what the Bible means. Among the earliest Christians, the prevailing type of interpretation was what we call the *literal-allegorical method.* According to this mode of interpretation, one must first read the scriptural text with painstaking attention to every detail of language. This rather artificial, literal reading will certainly turn up some oddities of expression, which will then be the foundation for the allegorical interpretation that follows. Allegory means "saying one thing and meaning another," and many ancient readers of the Bible assumed that that was exactly what the biblical authors had done. The task of the interpreter, then, was to unravel the code and find out what the writer really intended to say.

An example of this kind of interpretation would be Clement of Alexandria's treatment of the parable of the Good Samaritan, from his little treatise, *What Rich Man Is Saved?* The parable, he notes, illustrates the commandment, "You shall love your neighbor as yourself." A man falls among brigands and is left for dead along the roadside. A priest and a Levite pass by without helping, but a Samaritan, a potential enemy, stops and rescues the man. "Which of these three," says Jesus, "do you think, was a neighbor to the man who fell into the hands of the robbers?" The lawyer with whom Jesus was speaking replied, "The one who showed him mercy" (Luke 10:36-37).

Most of us would read these verses in a relatively loose way. The word "neighbor," we might reason, represents a reciprocal relationship. If the Samaritan proved to be the wounded man's neighbor, that was because he had recognized the wounded man as *his* neighbor. Thus, Jesus means that anyone in need is a neighbor whom we are to love as ourselves. But that is not a *literal* reading in the technical sense. The commandment tells me to love my neighbor as myself; the parable gives the title "neighbor" not to the person who needed help, but to the person who gave it. This means that my neighbor is the person who has helped me in my greatest need, that is, Jesus himself. Or so Clement argues.

In this way, the meaning of the passage becomes something rather different from what it might seem at first sight; it is an *allegory,* with the Samaritan signifying Jesus. Such an interpretation of the passage may seem very odd to us, but this general type of interpretation (with many variations of detail) was quite usual among the earliest Christians. As usual with a complex methodology, most interpreters did not bother to work through the whole process from literal to allegorical interpretation every time they took a text in hand, but they did work in this general framework. Thus, Paul, in Galatians 4:21-31, fashions an allegory out of the story of Sarah and Hagar, the two women by whom Abraham first had children. Hagar represents Mt. Sinai and the Jerusalem of this world, whose children are in bondage to the Law; Sarah represents the Jerusalem that is to come, whose children have been freed from Law by the Gospel. Paul does not bother to lay a foundation in literal exegesis here but goes straight to the allegorical interpretation.

In a similar way, the author of the Epistle to the Hebrews treats Melchizedek allegorically: "Without father, without mother, without genealogy, having neither beginning of days nor end of life, but resembling the Son of God, he remains a priest forever" (Heb. 7:3). How does he know such things about Melchizedek, who is barely mentioned in Genesis 14? He does not bother to tell us, but it is easy enough to reconstruct, once one knows how the literal-allegorical method works. In the Scriptures of Israel, the name of a king's father and/or mother is usually given, but Genesis is silent on such matters with regard to Melchizedek. Accordingly, there is an oddity in the letter of the text, upon which one is called to build the allegory. If the text omits vital information, that suggests that there is more to this passage than meets the eye. And that is all that the interpreter needs to set an allegory in motion.

Grammatical Interpretation

The literal-allegorical mode of interpreting Scripture was the basic pattern through more than half of Christian history. It seemed, however, as if one could produce almost anything out of Scripture in this way. By the time of the Reformation, literal-allegorical interpretation had already largely given way to another technique, sometimes called the *grammatical method*. According to this way of interpreting Scripture, one looks not at the letter (as in the literal method) but at slightly larger units of language and tries to adhere as closely as possible to the plain and obvious meaning of the phrases. The usual assumption was that this plain and obvious meaning could then be applied directly to the life of the contemporary Christian community.

Problems arose here, too, however. Luther, for example, discovered that the plain and obvious sense of Scripture could produce contradictions. For Luther, the central truth of the Gospel was Paul's proclamation of salvation by the grace of God alone, without any consideration of a person's merit or lack thereof. Certain books of the New Testament, however, such as Hebrews and James, seem to contradict or limit this teaching. Luther, accordingly, relegated them to a position of lesser authority.

Other kinds of problems arose because the plain and obvious sense could be understood in more than one way. The First Epistle to Timothy gives qualifications for people to be ordained as bishops (or overseers) and deacons (or servants) in the church, while the related Epistle to Titus gives qualifications for the office of presbyter (or elder). These passages subsequently gave rise to long arguments in Britain between Presbyterians, who held that the offices of bishop and of presbyter were one and the same, and Episcopalians, who held that they were different.

Historical-Critical Interpretation

The grammatical method, accordingly, gradually gave place to yet another kind of interpretation, the *historical-critical method*. This method has dominated modern scriptural scholarship down to the present. It emphasizes that language means something only in context; if the context changes, so will the meaning of the language. Thus, the author of 1 Timothy and Titus was intent on establishing certain standards for the Christian ministry---standards which would assure that only respectable and rather conservative males were appointed to office. No doubt, the author had a variety of reasons for this, not least of which was that he wanted Christians to present an unexceptionable appearance to the people around them, so that others would find it hard to justify persecuting them. He certainly did not intend to lay a foundation for civil and religious warfare in England and Scotland. He may not even have cared particularly whether there were to be three orders of ministry or two, or even one.

The historical-critical method implies that the concerns of the biblical authors might have been rather different from those of modern Christians and that we cannot force them to speak directly to our circumstances. They are far removed from us, after all, in terms of time and space and culture. If we want to understand what they meant to say, we must understand how they lived and what difficulties they encountered and how they viewed their world. Then it may be that we shall find analogies in our own experience, so that we can apply their words to our needs.

Today, some biblical interpreters feel that the historical-critical method, too, has had its day and that we must go on to yet other types of interpretation. They fault it because it seems unable to make the Scriptures truly contemporary. However this may be (and no resolution is yet in sight), it is clear enough from the brief sketch I have given that the church's freedom in interpreting the Scriptures has been very great indeed. Not only has the church changed its mind about the meaning of specific passages from time to time, but it has also actually changed its whole way of approaching and dealing with Scripture. It may seem to some that this makes the Bible a mere plaything of the church. And yet, without some such effort at interpretation, the Bible could not speak at all in the new circumstances of each succeeding age.

Scripture as Judge of the Church

The Bible is thus dependent on the community of faith both for its origins and for its continuing ability to speak to the faithful under changing circumstances. At the same time, I want to affirm that the Christian community is also dependent on the Bible for its life and integrity. I have already noted that the canonization of the Scriptures was no one-way street; if the churches set certain books apart as Scripture, that was at least partly because the books themselves made a deep and lasting impression on their Christian readers. The same kind of interdependence holds in the matter of interpretation. The church must interpret the Bible so that the Bible will have a living voice in each age, but the church must not use the process of interpretation merely to justify what the church itself happens to be.

Once Christians have accepted the Bible as embodying the Word of God—the message that lies at the heart of our existence as Christians—from then onward the Bible has a certain authority over against the church. The church, as the living community of faith, will always go on changing and developing, but not every change and development will be good. As a community of believers, we have the power not only to realize anew the meaning of our faith but also to betray it by accepting false notions of the world or of God. This possibility has existed throughout the history of the church. Paul, in his New Testament letters, was already recalling his recent converts to the true meaning of their faith:

> I am astonished that you are so quickly deserting the one who called you in the grace of Christ and are turning to a different gospel....Even if we or an angel from heaven should proclaim to you a gospel contrary to what we proclaimed to you, let that one be accursed!" (Gal. 1:6, 8)

What check can there be to show us when we have departed from the Gospel in this way? The church must always be able to show continuity with its first days and to prove that it is preaching the same Gospel. A church that breaks radically with its scriptural foundations will no longer be a community of Christian faith but something else. This is why reformers in every age appeal to Scripture in attacking what they see as the errors of existing church life. It makes no difference in this respect that the Bible itself does not always speak with one voice. There is always in Scripture that which calls the church into question, which judges the direction it has taken and finds its life incomplete.

We may take as an example the issue of Christian involvement in the political affairs of the world. From at least the time of Constantine the Great (the early fourth century) onward, the church has been deeply entangled with government. Before that, of course, it had little voice, since it was an illegal organization and was well-advised to keep a low profile. After Constantine legalized Christianity, however, and embraced it himself, Christians assumed more and more power in the running of the government; and there have been times and places where it has been entirely in their hands. The church as an institution has varied a great deal in how it has dealt with this relationship, ranging from wholehearted and uncritical approval of the secular authorities, to efforts that would have reduced secular government to a puppet of ecclesiastical authority, to attempts at ignoring the whole issue.

The entanglement between church and state has often been injurious to both, as in the Inquisition, the Crusades, or the witchhunts of Puritan New England. At other times, however, Christian involvement in politics has been the means of achieving notable good, as when St. Ambrose, bishop of Milan, forced the Roman emperor to do penance for his excessive and callous use of force, or when William Wilberforce led the battle to halt the slave trade. In America, the doctrine of separation of church and state has had equally mixed results. It means that some Christians never think about the possibility that their religion might have something to say about the ways of the world, but it also means that we have enjoyed an unusual degree of freedom to think and believe as we choose.

What does the Bible have to do with this whole question? It lines up quite clearly on both sides of it, and that is exactly its great value. It provides a weapon in the hands of those who fight all kinds of abuses, those arising from the entanglement of church and state and also those arising from their separation. To the person who denies that religion has anything to do with politics, the Bible speaks in the voices of Amos or James and says clearly that what religious people claim to believe about the love of God, they must prove in their actions. To the Christian who is elated by the joys of wielding power and who wants to impose the will of God (as he or she sees it) on the world by force, the Bible speaks in the voice of Jeremiah or Paul and says that the Lord looks on the heart and not merely on some external conformity.

The church, then, is subject to the Bible, just as the Bible is dependent on the church. The Scriptures that originated and were canonized in the community of faith now serve to judge the community, since they embody its earliest or best perception of its own essence. But why should this be so? Is this not a cumbersome way of managing things? Would not God have done better to establish some more direct chain of authority to convey the will of God to us? Thus far, I have tried to describe what does in fact happen in Christianity, but we need to take another step at this point and ask whether there is some reason why it must be this way—some reason deep in the very nature of the creation in which we live.

Scripture Breaks Down
the Walls Around Us

The fundamental fact of this creation is finitude. This world exists in coordinates of space and time. The concreteness of such an existence contributes much beauty and purpose to our lives, but it also limits us sharply. We know and understand, so to speak, only what is under our noses. Both as individuals and as communities, then, we are always in danger of finding ourselves locked into what we might call "the prison of the present." I have watched a two-year-old child working a puzzle and heard her proclaim loudly, "I can't do it," only an instant before setting the piece in place. So narrow is a child's present. As adults, we may find our horizons widened—but never infinitely.

Is there anyone who has not experienced some fear or despair or hope which subsequent experience proved completely false? Often, indeed, we impose such emotions on ourselves because we have overvalued things that turned out to be of little importance to us. At other times, we simply did not know enough to understand what was a serious challenge to us and what was not. Once we move on from the presence of fear or hope into the presence of fulfillment, we know more and can recognize whether our emotions were well founded or not. But this "moving on" is exactly what is difficult. The force of circumstance may compel us to move on, but if it does not, we may be left hanging a long time in a painful present of uncertainty.

In such cases, we cannot help ourselves. It requires the influence of some outside person or event to alter the situation and break us out of the prison of the present. William Blake once wrote of those who could not be saved "except by the advice of a friend." It is a common experience. The word from without touches a seemingly impenetrable problem and dissolves it—or at least clarifies it so that one can deal with it. Whether that "advice of a friend" comes in the form of the actual speech of a human companion or in other forms—human example, the experience of nature, the power of art, the in-breaking of inspiration—it takes an outside influence to break through the walls of space and time and knowledge in which we all live.

Communities are not fundamentally different in this respect from individuals. Their boundaries of space and time are wider, and within those limits there is more variety of thought and feeling. Yet the boundaries are there, and at times they constitute a true prison. How else can we explain why the preoccupations of one age and place so often seem absurd in another? Political suspicion between Protestants and Roman Catholics is pretty well dead in the United States. Why is it so bloodily alive in Ireland? Modern scholars find it difficult to discern real differences of belief between Orthodox Chalcedonian Christology (sanctioned at the Council of Chalcedon in A.D. 451) and that of the "heretical" Monophysites (condemned at the same time). Why did the verbal differences between them seem to justify such intense animosity fifteen hundred years ago? Presbyterians and Episcopalians may still differ seriously about the advantages of their respective polities. But why did they go to war over the matter in the seventeenth century?

It is our lack of perspective that causes us to mistake small questions for great ones, that makes us wilt before minor trials or march stupidly into the face of certain disaster. If we were not confined in this prison of space and time, where we can see only our immediate surroundings, we should perhaps be able to form a more just estimate of our situation. Yet to be delivered from it absolutely would mean that we were no longer human beings in the same sense. Perhaps the life of the heavenly Jerusalem will not be bounded in the same ways. Yet, if that life is to be a truly human life, it will be because we have experienced the reality of space and time.

Still, granted that both the individual Christian and the community live in a prison of the present and that we require outside intervention to free us from it, what does all this have to do with the Bible? The Bible belongs forever to the past. No one has added to it or subtracted from it for a long time, and it is unlikely that anyone will in the near future. Even when the canon first began to be formulated, most of the books that entered into it were already quite old, and their age was one of the reasons for including them. This means that the Bible always stands outside our present.

It is not always easy to see this. Christian communities develop certain traditions of reading Scripture; they domesticate it in this way so that nobody will be surprised by it. Much of the time, as we read Scripture, we see nothing but that traditional interpretation, and we hear nothing new or unusual. Yet the very fact that these are documents of the past means that the appearance of sameness and predictability can never be altogether true. The past was different from the present, sometimes quite dramatically so. When we read ancient documents, we are looking out of the window of our prison onto a different landscape of human existence. And when we read them well, they begin to speak to us and even to offer a critique of life as we think we know it. It is this experience that breaks down the walls around us.

God, of course, has not ceased to deal with us in a variety of ways. God speaks through preaching and through liturgy, through counselors and through enemies, through casual comments of chance acquaintances and through direct inspiration, when an idea "comes to us from without." God spoke to the faithful of antiquity in the same ways. The advantage we possess is that through the Bible we have access to their experience with God in their worlds in addition to our own experience with God in ours. The result is an extraordinary and unpredictable opening-up of our perspectives.

Without the Bible, the church can only degenerate into something no thoughtful person would care to be associated with: a tyrannical means of controlling society, it may be, or a series of squabbling sects, each developing in a different direction but all with equal rigidity. Without the Bible, we as individuals, too, would be encouraged to develop an increasing rigidity and immobility, locked into the prisons of our present by the inability to recognize that there is anything beyond. The Bible, then, is the principal condition of life and growth for the faithful, for it forbids us to suppose that our present is the sum total of human life under God.

Scripture as
the Beginning of Pilgrimage

Someone may ask, "Why should all this be necessary? Why all this talk of movement and change? Is this really a feature of Christian existence?" I must admit at once that movement and change are of no particular value in themselves. All churches and all individual Christians are changing all the time, whether consciously or not, and the change may as easily be for the worse as for the better. The church has certainly degenerated in particular times and places to the point where it has hardly deserved to be called the church. The important point about change, however, is that without it no growth is possible.

And growth is indeed an indispensable element of Christian existence. Can any of us claim, right now, just as we are, to be all that God wills for us? Merely to pose the question is enough for us to recognize its absurdity. As fit citizens of the kingdom of heaven, we shall all be rather different from what we are now, in ways that we cannot fully predict. "Beloved, we are God's children now; what we will be has not yet been revealed. What we do know is this: when he is revealed, we will be like him, for we will see him as he is" (1 John 3:2). Our future is largely unknown and unknowable, but it is certain that it will be different from our present. Insofar as we can see into it, we do so through Jesus; but even him we do not yet see "as he is."

In the second chapter of Acts, we encounter Peter preaching, as it were, the first Christian sermon. The many people converted by it responded by asking what they were to do. The first thing that Peter demanded of them was *repentance*. The Greek word that Luke used in his narrative, however, suggests something more than its

English equivalent. *Metanoia* suggests not only repentance from past sins but an entire change of perspective. This *metanoia* is not only the first step of a Christian life, but an ever-present requirement of it. "Here we have no lasting city," as the author of Hebrews (13:14) tells us, "but we are looking for the city that is to come." For now, we are all strangers and pilgrims. Whenever we seem to have settled down and found our true identity and come to the fulfillment of our lives, it is time to repent and take up the sacred journey once again.

In chapter three we demonstrated that the church is the practical authority for our Christian life. That is the way things work, at least, and there is nothing inherently wrong with it. Only a living and accessible authority, only the community of faith, can give an identity and norms and checks that are fully relevant to our present situation. Yet the church as authority has the weaknesses that go with its strengths. As a living and accessible community, it lives too much in the present and suffers the corresponding failure of perspective. Then it must be brought to repentance. The walls of its prison must be broken down; new light must shine in, and new visions of reality be unveiled.

The church, then, without the Bible is an uncertain voice, at best. The Scriptures, a voice out of the past, arise to correct, to judge, to discipline, and to encourage the church. Hearing the message of the Gospel anew, the church gives voice to it in the words of today. Yet, with time, those too will harden into a new prison and will need to be replaced by the language of another today. "O that today you would listen to his voice! Do not harden your hearts, as at Meribah, as on the day at Massah in the wilderness, when your ancestors tested me" (Ps. 95:7b-9).

Sometimes the individual Christian is put in a difficult spot by this duality of authorities. Sometimes we may hear the Bible speaking one thing and the church another. In such a situation, if with all humility we are persuaded that our individual perception is correct, we must decide for Scripture. It is in this way that the church learns to hear the Word afresh. The bearer of the Word under such circumstances sometimes meets the fate of those who bore it in antiquity and had to face rejection and even persecution. Still, it is the object of the Gospel to move us toward the Kingdom, not to make us content with the life of the present. Without such conflict we should likely stagnate and never know more of God's will for us than what we happen to know at this moment.

To be citizens of the Age to Come, we will have to change and grow----in understanding as well as in our actions. We have a journey, a pilgrimage, ahead of us. The Bible helps us recognize that our present is not sufficient. It points us toward the road into the future.

Chapter 5

Scripture's World and Ours

We have seen that the Bible and the church are coordinate authorities, under God, for the Christian life. Neither is sufficient by itself. The Bible cannot give us a single sense of identity or a single set of norms because it does not always agree perfectly with itself. It cannot serve as an immediate check on our progress because it is not a living, accessible voice. The church, on the other hand, can supply these needs, but it has a tendency to become caught in its own present and to degenerate into something less than what God wills for humanity. When this happens, the Bible serves as the church's judge, calling it to repentance and a new understanding of God's purpose.

It may seem that this is a very discouraging picture of the church, but that is so only if we have begun by expecting too much of the church in the first place. The works and words, the people and institutions of this created order are not perfect in the way that God is; they are not eternal, infinite, and complete as they stand. The possibilities with which God has endowed the human species are but slowly being revealed, as one age or society or culture succeeds another. The one truly unfaithful thing is to become static. We may imagine God as unchanging because in eternity all things seem somehow to be present at once. Time, however, as Plato said, is a *moving* image of eternity. If we hope for some kind of perfection that is appropriate for us, we can move toward it only by changing and growing. It must be a pilgrimage for us.

This means that every Christian community is incomplete and unfinished, just as every individual is. The Bible, therefore, in every age will witness that we have yet more to do and to become. No doubt the Bible will sometimes disclose astonishing and unthought-of things to us, changing our point of view quite radically, as happened in the case of St. Augustine and of Luther. But how does this happen? How do we help the Bible speak to us in this way? How, in short, do we get from the world of the Bible to where we are now?

We are asking about how we can interpret the Bible in our own day. As we have seen, the church has employed a variety of methods over the centuries, and none of them can be considered final. The whole question of the principles of interpretation (a field known as "hermeneutics") has become very important in recent years as people recognize its difficulty. In one short chapter we can hardly discuss the issue in all its subtlety. But it should prove beneficial if we set out, in plain terms, the principles that this study implies; for the way we interpret Scripture will determine, to a great extent, what we get out of it. If we were interested, for example, only in history, in "what actually happened," we should not bother looking for theology; in fact, we might even discount everything theological. On the other hand, if we were looking only for "proofs" of a certain theological position, we would discount or explain away the things that seem irrelevant or contradictory.

Previously I have argued that the most important function of biblical authority is to produce *metanoia,* a transformation of understanding and life. Interpretation, as I understand it, helps the Bible fulfill that function today. How, then, should we approach the Bible to facilitate this change of perspective? The first step is to recognize that the Scriptures we study really do stand outside our present; they are not just uttering the familiar verities and tired platitudes that we have been hearing all our lives. If they seem to be trite, the fault is in us, because we have not really heard them aright.

Discovering the Distance

Over the ages, the churches have adopted various ways of ensuring that the Scriptures would be heard to speak things strange and new. Literal exegesis was one such method, but it seems very artificial by modern standards. In our own time, we have another means to ensure this same end, and I think it is a better one. I mean the modern, historical-critical study of Scripture. The presupposition of this study is that the biblical writings belonged originally to another age and meant certain things in terms of that age. If one could recover enough information about the way people lived and thought in the time when this or that book was written, one would see that the meaning had to do first and foremost with their particular situation, not ours.

Historical-critical scholarship is particularly conscious of what separates us from the people of antiquity—of the ways in which life and the world have changed over the last two to three thousand years. When scholars set Scripture back into its original setting, the people, places, and events of Scripture sometimes seem remote and irrelevant to our modern condition. Consider, for example, the Immanuel prophecy: "Look, the young woman is with child and shall bear a son, and shall name him Immanuel" (Isa. 7:14). This passage is often read around Christmastime, and we have a sense of immediate attachment to it. Referring it to the birth of Jesus, we find in it a direct connection with our faith as Christians and even with our calendar of holidays. The historian, however, reads the verse in the context of the whole chapter and of the events of Isaiah's lifetime, and finds that it was really a political prophecy: namely, that before the child soon to be born could exercise moral choice, the threat to Judah from its enemies to the north would have evaporated. The message turns out to be different from what we had expected—and perhaps in a disappointing way.

Yet it is worth a certain number of disappointments if only the Bible can be freed from the burden of false familiarity. For as long as that familiarity lulls us into inattention, we shall never hear anything new that might prompt us to *metanoia,* to a change of perspective. Historical-critical scholarship, paradoxically, ensures the newness of Scripture by showing us that it is really very old. What is important is that it belongs to another age and place—indeed, to a variety of ages and places. The ideas and points of view expressed in it, then, are not literally new, but they are strange to us, living in our place and time. That understanding is all that is necessary. Once we begin to learn how God dealt with our predecessors, we shall never be able to suppose that the faith and life of our own experience are God's final and complete will for us.

To some extent, any approach to the Bible that enhances its "strangeness" will fulfill the same function. The historical-critical method, however, has the advantage of being based on the fundamental nature of written works. Writing has proved to be a great benefit to humanity by enabling us to preserve the record of events and human reflection over long spans of time. And yet it has been a mixed blessing. As Plato observed, writing cannot answer questions except by repeating itself. It is easy for the written word (as for the spoken word) to convey misimpressions or to be opaque or ambiguous; yet we have hardly any other means to clarify its meaning when this is so. In a live conversation, the interchange of dialogue helps to bring speaker and hearer to the point of mutual understanding. But the written word is, so to speak, an amputated conversation, lacking some important parts.

The written word lacks not only the live interchange between speaker and hearer but also the immediate common context that makes a live conversation possible. The participants in such a conversation share a common location in time and space. Usually they also share a common culture, with all its mutual expectations and presuppositions. What is perhaps most important, they are apt to share some common purpose or occasion which has brought them together to talk. In the case of the written word, these elements of context are gradually lost. An office memo may be very much like a conversation in the sense that the shared context is still immediate. Take it out of the firm or institution in which it was written, however, and it may be quite unintelligible to outsiders. A scholarly book on the Gospels written fifty years ago may have made perfect sense to its contemporary audience because it concentrated on questions which then concerned all scholars of the Gospels. The same book may make strange reading for a scholar today, simply because the scholarly community has changed and become interested in different questions and methods.

Finally, a book that becomes a classic and continues to be read for generation after generation will gradually cross the boundaries of culture. Its readers will change quite radically over the centuries—from elitists, perhaps, to democrats; from agrarian to industrial people; from Greek-speaking Jewish Christians to English-speaking undergraduates of no particular religious identity. No one noticed just when things changed, but changed they are. And what does the modern English-speaking person know of life as a Palestinian villager in the first century A.D.? How can we step back into the minds and lives of Jesus' original audience? How can we have any notion of the effect of his words on them? They were village people, for the most part, who lived as subjects in a world of great empires, paying taxes to foreigners, hoping that this year's harvest would last until next year's, that the Roman governor would not behave too tyrannically, that there would be no civil war this year. We are mainly people of the metropolis, citizens, not subjects, living in a society (though not a world) of great wealth, with more fear of crime or terrorism than of famine or imperial misgovernment.

The written word, then, is a great blessing which brings with it a serious problem, and what I have said of the written word in general applies in all respects to the Bible. While Jesus was speaking to a Palestinian audience, there was an intimacy of context that was no longer possible when his words were repeated later on. When his words were reduced to writing, it was done not for Palestinian villagers but for urban people who spoke Greek. Already we have here a considerable stretching out of the original context. When the Greek books are then translated, more than a millennium later, for people who speak English—a people and a language that did not even exist in Jesus' time—we have carried matters very far indeed.

The situation, however, is far from hopeless. Even if we cannot stand on the mountain and *be* Jesus' original hearers, we can learn enough about them to begin to empathize with them and to hear the words of Jesus in something like their original sense. Perfection will never be possible in this effort, but it is not necessary, either. It will be enough that our perspective is widened beyond our own experience. The means for making this approximation are the methods of historical-critical scholarship: the study of ancient languages and literature, comparison with other ancient documents and physical remains, careful analysis of the historical and religious statements in Scripture itself.

Not everyone, of course, can enter into this task to the same degree. We differ in disposition, in enthusiasm, in the freedom to pursue studies, and so forth. The most basic results of scholarship, however, become available to everyone through good annotated editions of Scripture, through commentaries, and through introductions to the Old and New Testaments. These help us make the imaginative leap into another world, where we may expect to hear surprising and unexpected things. Always, we must be on the lookout for what is strange and perplexing, for these are our windows on another view of the world.

Two Examples

Consider, for example, the first verse of the Gospel according to St. John: "In the beginning was the Word, and the Word was with God, and the Word was God." This is a strange statement, for many reasons. To begin with, why the "Word"? One may discern a relationship with the first chapter of Genesis, where God does most of his creating by word alone, and that would certainly be right. But a full understanding of the matter will lead us into a world of thought, shared by Greek philosophers and Jewish teachers of Wisdom, that sets the universe in a light rather different from our half-conscious modern empiricism. The Greek term *Logos,* translated "Word" in most English New Testaments, also means "reason" and "rationality," as well as a good many other things. The author of the Fourth Gospel is not only talking about the creative word of God in Genesis 1, but also about the mind of God, which is somehow God's own self.

Some Greek thinkers taught that our tangible, physical world is only a pale copy of the true reality, which exists unchanged and unchanging in eternity. The Jewish thinker Philo carried this line of thought over into his interpretation of Genesis and spoke of that real world as existing in the mind of God; in creating our world, God copied from that more perfect model. Some Jewish teachers had already been speaking about God's Sophia, or Wisdom, a being who was virtually identical with God but who could at least be thought of as distinct from him. Perhaps she was the repository of this preexistent and superior reality. The *Logos* of John seems to be the same as the Sophia of these earlier writers.

Here, then, we are on foreign ground indeed. The author of the Fourth Gospel sees a world which is turned on its head, from our point of view. We think of the tangible as the real. Both the irreligious and religious among us are apt to be uncomfortable with notions of the supernatural. Sometimes we even reduce God to a kind of pale worker of psychological illusions. For the Fourth Evangelist, however, the real situation is just the reverse. True, the physical world is important for him: "The Word," he says, "became flesh" (John 1:14). It is the only world, for the most part, that is immediately accessible to us, through which we may come to understand what is more real. Yet it is not "reality" par excellence. The place to begin a Gospel, for him, is not in this world but in the preexistent reality of the *Logos* of God.

Another example of the strangeness of Scripture is the story of the Ark of the Covenant being moved to Jerusalem (2 Samuel 6). The ark was placed on an ox cart, with two men to attend it on the way. "When they came to the threshing floor of Nacon, Uzzah reached out his hand to the ark of God and took hold of it, for the oxen shook it. The anger of the Lord was kindled against Uzzah; and God struck him there because he reached out his hand to the ark; and he died there beside the ark of God" (2 Sam. 6:6-7). It is a strange reward for so well-intentioned a gesture. Uzzah meant only to steady the sacred chest and keep it from being damaged.

Once again, however, we find ourselves looking back at a different view of the world. Like many other ancient peoples, the ancient Israelites thought of holiness as a dangerous phenomenon. It was not primarily a moral quality, as we may think of it today, but a kind of power. Like electricity or natural gas, it might serve those who knew how to handle it correctly and were authorized for its use, but it could kill anyone who came into contact with it without the proper preparations. The question of Uzzah's intention was irrelevant.

We are told that David "was angry" at the incident. Was he angry at the Lord's injustice in killing Uzzah? I doubt it; there is no hint of that. He was angry, rather, because he, too, thought he was doing a pious act in bringing the ark to his capital city. If the Lord could kill Uzzah for his pious act, might he not also harm David and his people for theirs? It must have seemed that God had committed a breach of hospitality. David, accordingly, decided to test the powers of the ark to see whether they were good or bad. He left the sacred chest with the family of Obededom and waited to see what happened. Only after the household was seen to be prospering did David decide that it was safe to continue the process and bring the ark into Jerusalem itself. It was a very different understanding of holiness from ours.

But what is the result of studies such as these? Do they serve only to make the Bible remote and unintelligible? If these ancient people thought so differently from us, one is tempted to think that they were simply wrong. They were probably superstitious people who knew no better, and we have nothing to learn from them. It is true, of course, that we cannot simply go back to believing and behaving as they did. Individual beliefs and practices from antiquity may reappear in later ages; democracy, for example, was an ancient concept reborn in the eighteenth century. But when such items do reappear, they do so as parts of new and different societies, so that even the individual items are no longer quite the same. The democracy of antiquity would seem like a kind of oligarchy by our standards, even if its rationale was similar to ours.

The past, then, cannot simply be hauled into the present by main force. We cannot decree that sacred objects will again inspire the fear that the ark did, long ago—much less give them the intrinsic power to kill those who meddle with them. Nor can we alter the materialist bias of our age by a mere act of will; it would not be easy, even if we wished to do so, to begin thinking of the local power plant as a shadowy reflection of the "real" power plant in the mind of God. Yet we have received, in these two examples, a brief glimpse out of our present into other ways of perceiving the world. The remaining problem is how to translate this new perception into terms that make sense for us.

Finding the Continuities

The totally unfamiliar, of course, does not make sense. Only insofar as we can bring these new/old perspectives into touch with our own experience will we see how they can also alter our experience. I said earlier that the first step in interpreting the Bible is to recognize that it really does stand outside our present. Let the past be past, and let it be as strange to us as it really was. The second step, however, is to look for the continuities. They are there, in some places more clearly than in others—but that is no surprise. The continuities are there because the biblical authors and the modern Christian are concerned with the same things: the ways of God with humanity, in the context of this universe.

I do not wish to oversimplify the matter. I do not want to say that human nature is somehow the same, always and everywhere. We do share the most basic needs: food, shelter, love, beauty, identity; but these can be satisfied in a myriad of different ways. We are more conscious of this in the modern world, as a result of the vastly expanded horizons of modern life and of the anthropological studies that have brought human divergency to our attention. Paul once asked, "Does not nature itself teach you that if a man wears long hair, it is degrading to him, but if a woman has long hair, it is her glory?" (1 Cor. 11:14-15). With his limited knowledge of human variety, he must have thought that the answer was yes. Now we know that vast numbers of human beings over the ages would have been astonished at any such notion.

The continuity of "human nature" will not help us much in dealing with the beginning of John's Gospel, or with the death of Uzzah. I think there is another continuity, however, that will—the continuity of human reflection. Our experience may differ widely, and our interpretation of it certainly does so; but underneath it all, we can sometimes perceive that we are reflecting on the same pervading themes of human life. In the story of the ark, for example, we are confronted with a fundamental fact of human existence—the irrationality of power and of the limits it imposes. How many human deaths make sense? In most, to be sure, the power of God is less directly and explicitly involved. Yet in some sense the power of God is behind the very structure of this universe, whose creator we claim God is.

The limits that we sense all about us—those limits, that is, that we cannot possibly overcome or evade—are in some way expressions of God's power. Perhaps such power is not the aspect of God that we are most apt to stress in the twentieth century, but it remains as unavoidable as ever. Indeed, given the dismal prospects of famine and death that confront us as the century draws to a close, we should devote ourselves to some consideration of this attribute of God. The alternative may be that we will be caught unawares by disasters for which we have not a glimmer of understanding. Holiness, in a way, is one name for these limits, for the holy is that which is radically other than us and which stands beyond some decisive limit that we cannot pass. Holiness and power are not, then, so unrelated. We, too, can catch a glimpse of the matter; and if it causes us to fear or, like David, to be angry, that is no justification for turning our backs on it. It will not go away.

If the story of the Ark of the Covenant exposes us to the themes of power and holiness, so the introduction to John's Gospel deals with the related themes of power and rationality. Much of what happens to us in life seems to make no particular sense, and often it would be easier to believe that life is under the control of some irrational or arbitrary Fate than to believe in an all-wise and loving God. But the author of the Fourth Gospel proclaims the faith that God's *Logos,* God's Word, or Reason, existed in the beginning, and he goes on to claim that this *Logos* was God's agent in creating the universe. The implication is that, hidden somehow beneath the apparent randomness of life, one may discern God's plan and purpose.

Perhaps we are scarcely able to discern this plan and purpose, but we have been given a clue as to how and where to look for them. John's Gospel tells us that the *Logos* of God has become flesh in the historical human person of Jesus of Nazareth (John 1:14). His ministry, suffering, death, and resurrection set the pattern for all human life, for in them God's purpose for us is revealed. It is a bold claim to say that the *Logos* of God could be incarnate in a single, particular human being. It is an even bolder stroke to suggest that somehow the suffering and death that appear to us to be the ultimate irrationalities of human experience may actually play a part in God's loving *Logos,* God's plan and purpose for us.

John may have spoken in terms that were particular to his own age and to its philosophical and religious speculations, yet he was dealing with issues no less important to us than to his contemporaries. To say that the one who died on the cross is the actual agent of creation is to say that God's purpose for us is not defeated by death but furthered. To say that the savior of the world is also its creator means that our salvation does not make us something other than human but is rather a completion and fulfillment of the humanity which is God's original gift to us. John's concerns are thus continuous with ours in the sense that, like us, he is reflecting on the relationship between our beginning and our end; and he finds the clue to that mystery in the person of Jesus.

Once we find the element of continuity between him and us, we shall find that he has much to say to us. So, too, with the rest of Scripture. If we begin by allowing the text to speak in its own language about the concerns of the day when its author first wrote, we shall find that it speaks to issues that are no less important to us today. Indeed, sometimes a particular passage will compel us to reconsider things we had forgotten about, such as the tension between God's love and God's holiness, and between the apparent irrationality of created existence and the rationality that we human beings long to find mirrored there.

The Danger of Shortcuts

To insist on a two-stage method of interpreting Scripture may seem a bit overcomplicated to some. Yet any attempt to short-circuit this approach will lead to disappointing or even misleading results. If we ignore the historical and cultural distance between us and the biblical writers, we will merely be perplexed at the multitude of superficial oddities in their writings. In trying to make sense of these oddities by reference to our own rather different experiences, we will either misinterpret them or find that they are irrelevant to most modern Christians. Take the example of the ark; since we know of nothing strictly comparable to it, we may conclude that it was utterly singular in its ability to kill those who touched it. Since the ark itself no longer exists, one can, fortunately, forget about that sort of threat to one's existence; it is no longer a concern for us. In the process, the whole point of the story about the relationship between power and holiness is lost.

Perhaps it is easier to see the absurdities of such interpretation when it is applied to something other than Scripture. The anthropologist Laura Bohannan once tried narrating the plot of *Hamlet* to some West African people whose culture was very different indeed from that of Elizabethan England. The results, as these people tried to make sense of the story in their own terms, provide a graphic illustration of how our ordinary biblical interpretation might look to a person able to view it from outside our own cultural milieu. Here is a brief excerpt from her account:

"The great chief (that is, Claudius) told Hamlet's mother to find out from her son what he knew. But because a woman's children are always first in her heart, he had the important elder Polonius hide behind a cloth that hung against the wall of Hamlet's mother's sleeping hut. Hamlet started to scold his mother for what she had done."

There was a shocked murmur from everyone. A man should never scold his mother.

"She called out in fear, and Polonius moved behind the cloth. Shouting, 'A rat!' Hamlet took his machete and slashed through the cloth." I paused for dramatic effect. "He had killed Polonius!"

The old men looked at each other in supreme disgust. "That Polonius truly was a fool and a man who knew nothing! What child would not know enough to shout, 'It's me!'" With a pang, I remembered that these people are ardent hunters, always armed with bow, arrow, and machete; at the first rustle in the grass an arrow is aimed and ready, and the hunter shouts "Game!" If no human voice answers immediately, the arrow speeds on its way. Like a good hunter, Hamlet had shouted, "A rat!"

I rushed in to save Polonius's reputation. "Polonius did speak. Hamlet heard him. But he thought it was the chief and wished to kill him to avenge his father...."

This time I had shocked my audience seriously. "For a man to raise his hand against his father's brother and the one who has become his father—that is a terrible thing...."

I nibbled at my kola nut in some perplexity, then pointed out that after all the man had killed Hamlet's father.

"No," pronounced the old man.... "If your father's brother has killed your father, you must appeal to your father's age mates: *they* may avenge him. No man may use violence against his senior relatives."

One excerpt can give but a pale impression of the overall confusion wrought in the story by Bohannan's listeners. They did not believe in ghosts or in any kind of personal immortality. The appearance of Hamlet's father's ghost, then, had to be an omen sent by a witch. Madness and drowning, too, can only be the work of witches, who must be male relatives of the victims. Hamlet, therefore, must have been bewitched by Claudius himself, who was thus responsible for all the tragedy ensuing, including his own death. Ophelia was done in by her brother Laertes, who wanted to sell her body to other witches. In the end, the audience was sure that it had understood the story far better than the narrator.

One elder said to her:

> "You tell the story well, and we are listening. But it is clear that the elders of your country have never told you what the story really means. No, don't interrupt! We believe you when you say your marriage customs are different, or your clothes and weapons. But people are the same everywhere; therefore, there are always witches and it is we, the elders, who know how witches work...."

At another point, when her audience had just made some major revision in the story, Bohannan remarks, *"Hamlet* was again a good story to them, but it no longer seemed quite the same story to me."

Bohannan's audience was unwilling to believe that sixteenth-century England could really have been so different from their own culture. As a result, they could not hear anything really new from the story but remade it so that it would not challenge their own presuppositions. It is easy for us to see the absurdity of the process when someone from outside our culture does it with one of our own classics. But it is the same thing we do with the Scriptures if we do not first allow them to belong to their own place and time; we deprive the Scriptures of their power to produce *metanoia* by confronting us with what is genuinely strange to us.

The proper method of interpreting Scripture, then, first requires us to locate the text in the original context in which it was written. We can do this only approximately, but even an approximation will be enough to help us see the text in a different light. The second step is to locate the continuities between the text and ourselves—continuities that will be found mainly on the plane of human reflection on experience. At this point, the dialogue between author and reader—a dialogue made difficult by extreme distance—can be renewed, and we can begin to learn from Scripture.

When I say that this is the "proper" way to approach Scripture, however, I mean this in terms of our own day. As I have already pointed out, Christians have approached the Bible with a great variety of interpretative methods and theories. No one who reads much in ancient exegesis, I think, can say that our predecessors were all entirely wrong-headed in the way they understood Scripture. For them, as for us, the Bible was able to say new and unheard-of things. Like them, however, we must approach Scripture from within our own culture. We have become conscious of the historical and cultural distance between us and antiquity, and I do not think that we can ever ignore it again successfully. Time and again, we shall find it necessary to come to terms with the critique "But that is not what it meant originally."

Inspiration and the Word of Truth

How, then, can we lay down such definite rules for our age and still admit that the interpretation of the Bible in the past was not entirely wrong, or that it may even have been equally satisfactory in its own time? Here, we must turn to a concept that has always been important for the Christian understanding of the Bible, the concept of *inspiration*. I have not used the term much in my discussion of the authority of the Bible because I think it misleads many people who take it to signify much more than it really does. Many people even suppose that one cannot believe that Scripture is inspired unless one also believes that it is completely inerrant. In actual fact, the two concepts have nothing to do with each other.

"Inspiration" means "filling with Spirit." It is not only a religious term but also an artistic one. A great piece of music or literature or painting may be recognized as "inspired," by which we mean that it appears to express something of more than human origin.

If I should claim to be inspired, I might say that these words I have written are not only the result of my own thought but that they have, in part, come to me from without. In other words, I have received them as a gift rather than working them out solely by my own labors and talents. Whether my claim is true or not would be for others to judge. If the results are utterly pedestrian, others would be apt to say, "The poor man has deceived himself." On the other hand, if other people, too, are struck by the newness or the exceptional truth of what I have written, they might well agree with my claim. They might even be the first to christen my writing "inspired."

Inspiration is not a category that *easily* transcends culture. That is to say, it is not easy for a person of one place and time to recognize the inspiration of works wrought in another. Statues that the pagan Greeks regarded as inspired were sometimes thrown into limekilns by their

Christian descendants. And the works of art in Mexico and Peru that the Spanish conquerors melted down into ingots are beyond numbering. Yet inspiration has a way of asserting itself even across boundaries of culture and time. By the Renaissance, at least, Christians had come to appreciate the art of pagan antiquity. And modern museums covet pre-Columbian artifacts like the ones the Spanish once turned into coin. Inspiration is a candle that cannot be hidden permanently.

When we use the term *inspiration* in connection with the Bible, we mean something of the same sort. In this case, we speak of the Bible's ability to assert itself and carry its message beyond the boundaries of its own time and place. Why? Because it is not simply a human product, although it is truly and fully a human product. Through it, there speaks a voice of larger-than-human reality, whether of this created universe or of God.

It is possible that some inspirations speak with an evil voice, while others speak simply with the voice of "things-as-they-are." Christians, for example, may find it difficult to hear the voice of the one God in the cruel and bloody art of the Aztecs; I, at least, do. Yet even this art speaks of realities that we cannot altogether escape, as the Holocaust of our century demonstrates.

The Christian claim about the Scriptures is that in them we hear the Word of God. That means that, like all inspired works, the Bible gives a true account of the world. It need not be scientifically true, in detail, nor even historically accurate; but it must be true in the larger sense that it calls to our attention those things which are most significant in our universe and places them in a meaningful perspective. The Bible differs from other inspired works, not in that it is "more" inspired, but in that its inspiration, stemming from God the Creator, gives a fuller and truer perspective than that of any other single work.

To say that the Bible is inspired is to say that it speaks to us and will go on speaking despite every transformation of human experience. No matter how badly we interpret it or how little we expect of it, it will not lose the ability to break through to the mind and spirit of our age, because truth cannot be kept quiet forever. The inspiration of Scripture is a source of confidence, since it assures us that all does not depend on the correctness of our theory or our skillfulness of method. This does not relieve us, however, of the need to approach the Scriptures skillfully. The Bible will speak, with or without our help, but it will speak better if we learn to cooperate in letting it do so.

Let the Scriptures, then, first of all be themselves. Let us admit that here are words from another era that are now alien to us. Once we have done so, we will be able to see that, in their own terms and their own context, the biblical authors were dealing with the same issues that confront us—issues of faith and understanding that do not fade in a thousand years or in ten thousand. Who is God? What kind of world has God made? Who are we, human spirits and souls and bodies, who find ourselves in this world? What are the limits of our existence and our power, and what lies beyond them? Why is suffering a part of our lives? Why does this world not measure up to the best that we might hope of it? And why does it give us so much more than we could have asked? The mysteries of our existence remain with us; to grow in comprehension of Scripture will mean that we grow in the mysteries, too.

Chapter 6

Taking the Scriptures on Pilgrimage

Any book, like the present one, that discusses what the Bible is, is bound to have implications about the way in which we should read it. I assume that most readers of this book are interested in applying Scripture, not just in theorizing about it; therefore, I want to be clear about this matter. Let me begin by summarizing my conclusions thus far: The authority of the Bible is an earthly authority and therefore cannot be absolute. Absolute authority belongs to God alone; and even when speaking through Scripture, God does so in a way limited by the very nature of the written word and the created world within which it exists. For us as Christians, the Bible is only one of the authorities that give us guidance. Under God, it is coordinate with the church, whose living voice acts as the practical authority for Christians most of the time.

The great significance of the Bible, as we have seen, is that it stands outside the present in which the church and the individual Christian live. Both communities and individuals are apt to become imprisoned in their own times—in the cultures and presuppositions in which they live. The Bible, however, because it stands outside our present, always bears witness against us, showing that we are not all that we might be or that God has prepared for us to be. The authority of the Bible discloses itself in making us dissatisfied, in offering us new perspectives, in giving us the hope of a better fulfillment of God's will for our humanity. In short, it is authority for producing *metanoia* in us, so that we will leave our present stagnation and begin our pilgrimage toward the heavenly city again.

Because the Bible's authority is authority for *metanoia,* I have argued that the first step in interpreting the Bible is to acknowledge that it belongs to another age (or, rather, to other ages) and that it says things other than what we are used to hearing. Let the Bible first be as strange as it wants to be; only then can we hope to find the deeper continuities that unite it with us, and that may alter our perception of our present. But what does this mean in terms of practical directions? How should one begin to read in order to get these results?

Two Pieces of Advice

I need scarcely say that there are no simple instructions for producing *metanoia* and conversion—any more than there are simple instructions for how to grow up or how to love one's spouse or how to become a saint. My "simple instructions" will do no more than try to remove some barriers. My *first* piece of advice is this: When we feel that we understand and agree with everything we read, we should feel suspicious of ourselves. I do not mean that everything we find ourselves agreeing with in the Bible is somehow wrong; I don't even mean that we have necessarily misunderstood whatever we agree with. After all, we have all had some experience of God and life; we are not infants. We have come this far in our pilgrimage already, and we have learned some true things along the way. Yet if the Bible speaks *nothing* new to us, something is wrong. We must have closed our ears, or we have them so well plugged with the presuppositions of our culture or of our Christian community or piety or theology that everything else is being shut out. Only as long as the Bible is challenging us are we reading it fairly.

My *second* piece of advice is this: Those things in Scripture that seem odd or irrelevant or even threatening are likely to be things particularly deserving of our attention. Some of the most important themes of the Bible, to be sure, will certainly seem familiar to us all, either because they are mentioned often in the Bible itself or because they are frequent elements in Christian preaching and teaching. "Love your neighbor as yourself" is certainly an important theme of the Bible, and it may well sound familiar to us. The problem is that most of us read it as a truism and fail to connect it with our lives. Only when it becomes strange for us and we realize that we have not plumbed its depths will it begin to exercise real power over us. The familiar may become strange whenever we see it in a new light or realize that it has implications we had not previously guessed; and by becoming strange again, it regains the power it had lost by being familiar.

To be sure, not everything that seems strange is necessarily helpful. For one thing, a text may appear strange only because we are misreading it. In that case, the best thing to do is to get it straight again as quickly as possible, even if that makes the text pedestrian once again. For another thing, some parts of the Bible will always be harder to deal with than others. The story about Samuel hacking up King Agag "before the Lord in Gilgal" is certainly strange and disturbing, and it may therefore be worthy of our careful consideration. I would not recommend, however, that one adopt it as central to one's faith merely because it is so strange. Passages that strike us as strange are helpful because they are "ways into Scripture," since they are likely to challenge our preconceptions, but they will not all speak equally to my particular condition or yours. You should always be prepared to move on to another text if the one you are studying proves not to be fruitful.

Three Practical Rules for Reading Scripture

These two basic principles should govern all our reading: Beware of too much complacency in our understanding of Scripture and allow the surprises in the reading to direct our attention. Then we will find that Scripture, instead of confirming us in our present, urges us to move onward in our pilgrimage. Yet as I have noted, some passages of Scripture may seem strange to us merely because we are misreading them, and we should take some precautions against that. There are no rules guaranteed to keep us from misreading; after all, we are of this creation and no more infallible than the Bible itself. There are ways of going about our reading, however, that can minimize the mischief. Here, I should like to offer three rules: 1) read in context; 2) take advantage of what others know; 3) *after* following these steps, look within yourself for the source of the difficulty. Let me explain at more length.

Read in Context

By *reading in context* I mean both that we should read the Bible as a whole and also that we should read it, as far as we can, in terms of its original cultural and historical setting. The first step is easy to illustrate, for we are all aware of the mischief that can be done when people tear items out of context. There is an old story about a preacher at the turn of the century who took exception to current women's hairstyles. One Sunday he preached a sermon on a text which sounded like "Topknot, go down!" Afterwards, a member of the congregation challenged him, doubting that the Bible contained such a verse, and he cited Mark 13:15, which turns out to read, "Let him who is on the housetop, not go down..." (KJV).

If every wrenching of context were this absurd, there would, of course, be no danger in the process. Unfortunately, the practice of reading or quoting out of context can produce more plausible and harmful results. Take, for example, the treatment of divorce in Western Christianity over the past centuries. Jesus' words prohibiting divorce and remarriage are found in several different contexts in the Gospels; the most informative, perhaps, is that of the Sermon on the Mount (Matt. 5:31-32). Here, the words of Jesus fall into a series of statements in which Jesus revises the Law of Moses in the direction of greater rigor. In fact, he revises it to the point of making it nearly impossible to fulfill. In place of the commandment "You shall not kill," he declares that merely to insult another person is enough to send us to hell. In place of the commandment "You shall not commit adultery," he says that even to lust after a woman is equally sinful. Where the Law says not to swear falsely, Jesus says not to swear at all. Where the Law permits revenge in the interest of justice, Jesus commands nonresistance to evil, and so forth. At the very least, these commandments must strain human ability to the limit, and some of them, such as the commandment against lust, go beyond what the human will can control.

Christians have disagreed as to the interpretation of most of these passages. Most of them have set aside the prohibition of oaths; few take the words about insult with any seriousness. Yet Western Christianity has taken the words about divorce and remarriage, which fall in the middle of this series, and treated them, alone of all these declarations, in a fully literal way. This seems to me to be a serious misinterpretation of the passage, occasioned by removing it from context. The result has been to make remarriage after divorce a kind of unpardonable sin, where the context suggests rather that unbroken marriage is an ideal toward which we are to direct our lives.

Immediately before the prohibition of remarriage, we find these words: "If your right hand causes you to sin, cut it off and throw it away; it is better for you to lose one of your members than for your whole body to go into hell" (Matt. 5:30). Not only have the Christian churches refused to take this verse literally, but they would certainly be distressed if anyone were to mutilate himself or herself on account of it. Why, then, have the churches of the West insisted that the verses following must be radically different in character? Thus, the importance of *reading in context* becomes apparent when we realize what a significant difference it can make in our understanding of important verses.

If the immediate context is so important, there is also another context of equal significance, *the context of Scrip-*

ture as a whole. Here is a point that often escapes our attention. We call the Bible "the Word of God," and the fact that we use the singular ("Word," not "words") is hardly an accident. The Bible as a whole speaks God's message to us in a way that no isolated passage does or can. And every text of Scripture acquires its full meaning only as we begin to relate it to the larger whole.

Again, we may use the example of marriage. If we wish to understand Jesus' attitude toward divorce and remarriage, we must look at more than one passage. We should consider, for example, the story of the woman taken in adultery (John 7:53--8:11). It tells how some people came to Jesus with a woman who had been caught in the very act of adultery; they were on their way to stone her, as the Law commanded, but stopped to ask Jesus' word on the matter. His response was, "Let anyone among you who is without sin be the first to throw a stone at her." At this answer, the crowd gradually melted away. Finally, Jesus said to the woman, "Has no one condemned you?...Neither do I condemn you. Go your way, and from now on do not sin again."

This story is not an original part of the Gospel of John, but it has been hallowed by long use among Christians. What is more, it is thoroughly in accord with what we know of Jesus' behavior elsewhere. He associated with the unrespectable and sinful people of the time more than with the religious people. Indeed, on one occasion he spoke with a Samaritan woman who had lived with five husbands and was now living with a lover. He did not condemn her but offered her the water of life (John 4:7-30). It does not make sense to interpret Jesus' prohibition of divorce in such a way that the church becomes unforgiving where Jesus was willing to be forgiving. I don't mean by this that Jesus was indifferent to divorce, for it is clear that he labeled it as an evil. I only mean to show that he did not regard such offenses as an absolute barrier to association with him. If we consider the message of the Gospel as a whole in this matter, it will refute any rigorism which the Western churches have mistakenly drawn from isolated passages torn out of context.

We see, then, that the rule *read in context* means two things: first, be conscious of the immediate context of every passage; second, understand that every individual passage is subordinate to the message of Scripture as a whole, for it is only the whole which is justly to be called "The Word of God." *Read in context* also means one further thing—to be aware of what *kind* of material you are reading. Not every kind of writing is read in the same way, as we know from daily experience. If I sit down to read a lyric poem, I expect to find a short and compressed piece of writing, in which the connotations of words are as important as their basic meanings. Even the sounds and rhythms will be of great importance in conveying the meaning. I will need to read slowly and reflectively, letting my mind range over all the varied images which the words suggest and choosing those that seem to fit together in this particular work of art. On the other hand, if I open a gardening book to find out what I ought to be doing in my garden in Berkeley in May, I will be very irritated if I find that I must read it in the same way as a lyric poem.

The Bible contains a variety of literary types, and we can learn to distinguish between them and to expect of each one only what it is able to give. A narrative, for example, tells a story, and if it tells it well, it will leave the story open to a variety of interpretations—just as life itself is open to a variety of interpretations. Thus, the parables of Jesus are open to more than one way of understanding them. The same is true of the stories about Jesus in the Gospels. Take, for example, the narrative of Jesus' baptism. Matthew tells it in such a way as to stress Jesus' humble obedience to God's will. Luke minimizes the importance of the baptism itself in favor of the descent of the dove and the message of the heavenly voice. Mark, who tells it most simply, gives us very few hints as to how he understood it. All of these writers, however, have left the story open to some extent, so that we do not know whether this experience was primarily a turning point for Jesus himself or whether it was the first public attestation to his ministry. We do not know for certain how Jesus understood it, or what it meant to John the Baptist. We do not even know whether this story is primarily a tale of humility or a tale of exaltation. This is as it should be, for it is the business of narrative to provoke reflection, not to close the door on it.

Prophecy, on the other hand, has as its business the interpretation of events. The prophet, of course, cannot close the process of interpretation any more than the narrator, for both alike are inhabitants of this world in which nothing is final. Yet we read prophecy differently, for our concern here is not to know what happened in all its ambiguity, but to understand how the prophet made sense of the events. When the Babylonians captured Jerusalem and sent the people of Judah into exile, did it mean that God had chosen the Babylonians in preference to Israel? Did it mean that God was now indifferent to the chosen people? Did it mean that God had rejected Israel forever? And if so, was this because of their sins or for some other reason? To this, the prophets answer: It is indeed God's doing; but God punishes only in order to heal.

Poetry, laws, proverbs, exhortation, theology—all are to be found in Scripture, and each type of writing needs to be read in a slightly different way. But in truth, there is no need to analyze each type in detail in this book. We are all aware that different kinds of writing call for different kinds of reading, and we only need to be reminded that the Bible is not a monolithic whole but contains a variety of kinds of literature.

More could be said about reading the Bible in context, but my intention here is only to give an introduction to the matter. The point of it all can be summed up in one exhortation: Lift your eyes from the verse and look farther afield. Meaning comes from the way the parts fit together in a whole; if we see only the parts, we shall never get to the true meaning.

Take Advantage of What Others Know

The second rule for reading Scripture is to *take advantage of what others know.* Today, even those who devote their whole lives to the study of the Bible cannot hope to know everything there is to know about it. Thousands of commentators and scholars over the ages have contributed their insights and discoveries to the totality of accumulated knowledge on the subject, and it is now far beyond the point where any one person can hope to master it. Most of us, of course, know that we cannot even set such a goal for ourselves. This means that we must all be ready to learn from others, who know things we have not had time to learn. This is not to say that the learned are always right about everything they think they know. Scholars spend a great deal of time and energy disagreeing with one another, and they cannot all be right all of the time. Still, there is a great body of accumulated knowledge about Scripture that can clear up many misconceptions about its meaning.

Take, for example, the Revelation to John. On first reading it, one is perplexed and intrigued and perhaps also distressed. It is a vividly pictorial book that seizes the imagination. It is full of mysteries to catch our curiosity. And it has a strong strain of vengefulness that may seem radically un-Christian. If a specialist in the matter, however, shows us exactly what kind of writing this is and what circumstances called it forth, the whole book becomes more intelligible. We learn, in fact, that the book belongs to the class of apocalyptic writings, all of which are characterized by an extravagant use of pictorial imagery. Yet this imagery, which seems so obscure and recondite to us, was familiar to the ancient reader and relatively easy to interpret. We can recover enough of this ancient interpretation to show with some certainty what the concealed message of the book is. At the same time, comparison with other apocalyptic literature helps us understand the vengeful nature of the book. All apocalyptic books stem from times of dread and persecution, when there seemed to be little chance that even a remnant of the righteous might be saved. It is not surprising (even if it is still not fully in accord with the Gospel) that the righteous began to wish that a little harm might befall their persecutors.

This kind of explanation may make the Revelation seem less exotic and interesting than before—though it loses none of its imaginative power thereby. And this may seem to run contrary to my earlier principle that the strange and perplexing elements in Scripture are apt to be most useful to us. Yet we do not want to be misled into thinking that every surface oddity in Scripture is an entry point. Many things that seem strange at first glance will turn out to be explicable if we know enough about them. The knowledge of others, then, will help us distinguish the truly strange from what is merely the vestige of a different age or style.

It is not only the factual knowledge of others, however, from which we profit. Equally important is their insight. It sometimes happens that people with very little education may see more clearly and effectively into the meaning of a passage of Scripture than the best educated person among us. Knowledge does not always impart wisdom, and ignorance does not always prevent it. Of course, knowledge in itself is useful, as I have suggested. But there is something unique in each of us—the result of experience and attention. Each of us also stands in a slightly different place from everyone else in the world and therefore has a different perspective—something which enables each of us to see certain things uniquely well. Therefore, even if we all had the same knowledge, we should still need to pay attention to each other in interpreting Scripture, in the expectation that we shall learn from each other what we could never have recognized by ourselves.

The study of Scripture, then, should always have a communal element to it. Even the scholar alone in the study consults the writings of others and compares results with colleagues. There is a value for each of us in studying Scripture privately, where we can devote ourselves to it with little distraction. In the long run, however, there must also be an opportunity for coming together with others, through writing or in person, and for comparing our results with one another and learning from one another.

Look Within

My third and last rule for reading Scripture is that after we have done everything else, if there remain some difficulties and perplexities, we are to *look within ourselves* for the possible source of the trouble. It may appear that the Bible is saying strange and unheard of things. But perhaps it is not the Bible that is strange; perhaps it is I. I may have to be converted to a new way of thinking and living before the Scriptures will appear to make sense to me. This is a step which we shall take with some trembling and caution, as is certainly appropriate here. If we leap to this stage too quickly, without laying a thorough groundwork, we may fly off after some quite mistaken notion. Yet if we do not come to this point sooner or later, all our study of Scripture is in vain, for we shall never have found in Scripture that which is most valuable in it—its authority for *metanoia,* for a change of mind and heart.

Three Examples of Interpretation

In conclusion, let me append a few short examples to illustrate the whole process—briefly sketched, one from the Old Testament and two from the New Testament. First, we will deal with the story of Moses at the burning bush (Exod. 3:1-12). God has commissioned Moses to bring the people of Israel out of slavery in Egypt, and Moses has protested that he is hardly qualified for the job. Then God says to him:

> I will be with you; and this shall be the sign for you that
> it is I who sent you: when you have brought the people
> out of Egypt, you shall worship God on this mountain.
> (Exod. 3:12)

If we read this verse in its immediate context, it creates a very odd impression. Moses needed some kind of immediate reassurance as he faced an impossible task; God gave him a sign, but not the kind that would do him any present good. Instead, the sign was related to something that God would do *after* bringing the people out of Egypt, when Moses no longer needed a sign at all!

The verse seems so odd, in context, that some scholars have even suggested that it must be a mistake; but we have no authority for any other reading. And if we read it in the context of the whole of Scripture, we shall find that it is not altogether unique after all. Jesus, too, entered into the most critical stage of his life—his trial, passion, and crucifixion—with fear and trembling. If he foresaw his resurrection, the Gethsemane story suggests that it did not free him from genuine dread of what was coming. The final author or final editor of Exodus, then, may very well have meant this passage just as it stands, and it is for us to discover the point of the narrative.

Moses was sent into Egypt without any conclusive proof of God's will or presence. He had seen a burning bush (Exod. 3:2) that was not consumed—hardly in a class with the storm and fire that he would later witness on Mount Sinai; and he had received a few magic spells with which to impress the Egyptians. That was all. Like Jesus, he was not granted the ultimate security of knowing the outcome without suffering the labors. If I protest the inadequacy of this "sign" that God gave him, the judgment returns to rest upon me, for I am perhaps wanting something for myself that God would not allow even to Moses and Jesus. There is indeed something strange in this passage—fundamentally strange. It is that God gives his signs *after* they are no longer needed to bear us through our fear. If we wish to understand that, we shall have to change our way of looking at life and surrender much of our desire for security in order to follow where God leads. Instead of resolving our uncertainties, the Bible sends us on a new journey of discovery.

My *second* example comes from the Gospel of Mark:

> Then his mother and his brothers came; and standing outside, they sent to him and called him. A crowd was sitting about him; and they said to him, "Your mother and your brothers and sisters are outside, asking for you." And he replied, "Who are my mother and my brothers?" And looking at those who sat around him, he said, "Here are my mother and my brothers! Whoever does the will of God is my brother and sister and mother." (Mark 3:31-35)

Again, there is an obvious element of strangeness in Jesus' apparent rejection of his closest relatives. If we consult those who know something of family life in ancient Palestine, they will tell us that the strangeness is not merely superficial. The family was tightly knit among ancient as among modern Jews. The Ten Commandments direct us to honor father and mother; the Psalms praise harmony among brothers. Jesus' words, then, will have created an immediate, probably negative sensation.

If we look at these words in the context of Mark's Gospel, we will find that they come as the climax and conclusion of a section in which Jesus breaks all kinds of old ties and makes a new beginning. At the beginning of Mark 3, Jesus offended the religious leadership of the day so deeply that Mark claims they even plotted to kill him. Jesus then fled from the crowds that followed him everywhere, taking only his disciples with him. In a remote place he appointed twelve of them as an inner circle. The number of those appointed suggests that they were in the tradition of the twelve sons of Jacob, the beginning of a new Israel. The scribes then accuse Jesus of being an agent of Beelzebub, and he responds by rejecting the scribes absolutely—those who blaspheme against the Spirit can never be forgiven.

When we come to the passage about Jesus' family, it seems clear that it belongs in this series. Along with the old regime of nation and religion, Jesus cancels the old regime of family and replaces it with a new institution, the family of faith. The same idea is confirmed elsewhere in Mark, when Jesus says, "Truly I tell you, there is no one who has left house or brothers or sisters or mother or father or children or fields, for my sake and for the sake of the good news, who will not receive a hundredfold now in this age—houses, brothers and sisters, mothers and children, and fields with persecutions" (Mark 10:29-30). But does this mean that Jesus is simply abolishing the family? Perhaps not, for elsewhere in Mark's Gospel, Jesus criticizes the Pharisees for placing restrictions on the commandment to honor father and mother (Mark 7:9-13). Moreover, the witness of the New Testament as a whole shows a continuing reverence for family life among the early Christians.

Here, then, we come up against something truly strange and apparently contradictory: The Bible both commands reverence for the family and also rejects the claims of the natural family in favor of the family of faith. This creates a tension that we cannot resolve simply by formulating some new rule. If we say, for example, that we are to respect our families except when the needs of the church take precedence, we will still be unsure exactly what justifies granting such precedence to the church. It seems to me that in cases such as this, the Word of God in Scripture designedly leaves us poised between the two absolutes, without resolving our uncertainty, so that we will need to work through the issue many times during our lives; the resolution will differ in different circumstances. The Bible does not give us a single rule, but tells us to accept that we are living in a necessary tension.

My first two examples were both drawn from narrative contexts. For a final example, let me turn to another literary type, a theological statement, from Paul's Epistle to the Romans:

> There is therefore now no condemnation for those who are in Christ Jesus. For the law of the Spirit of life in Christ Jesus has set you free from the law of sin and of death. (Rom. 8:1-2)

This seems like a simple and straightforward statement that ought to mean the same thing to everybody. Paul believed in salvation by grace, not by human merit; and as a human being cannot earn salvation, neither can one defeat God's good purpose by one's sins. Accordingly, Paul held a kind of doctrine of "Once saved, always saved." Once we have entered into Christ, there can be no further question of condemnation.

Does this mean, however, that it no longer makes any difference what I do? Not at all. Paul's letters are full of exhortations to Christian people to stop doing evil and to do good works. We cannot enter here into the reasons Paul gives for this; suffice it to say that he still thought moral behavior was important. But why should it even be a problem? Does not Paul go on to say that "the law of the Spirit of life...has set you free from the law of sin and death"? Does this not mean that some quite new principle has taken over our life, so that we are no longer likely to sin? Not at all. Paul has just argued the reverse in the preceding chapter of Romans:

> I find it to be a law that when I want to do what is good, evil lies close at hand. For I delight in the law of God in my inmost self, but I see in my members another law at war with the law of my mind, making me captive to the law of sin that dwells in my members. (Rom. 7:21-23)

This statement seems to contradict the passage I cited in the first place. Paul is somehow maintaining that we live in a state of contradiction: "If Christ is in you, though the body is dead because of sin, the Spirit is life because of righteousness" (Rom. 8:10).

If we turn to the larger context of Scripture, we will not find much clarification. The Bible speaks plainly of God's power to save despite human sinfulness, and it also speaks clearly of the power of sin to destroy, even in the face of God's gracious appeal to humanity. Theologians have found it difficult to reconcile the two sides of Paul's thought and of the biblical witness, in part because it is scarcely possible to make simple, coherent sense of these contrary themes. Once again, then, we are forced back onto ourselves. If there is not some simple and rational solution to Paul's strange way of expressing himself, how else can we make sense of it?

Here I will reiterate the most important thing I have to say about the whole subject of this book. *The Bible makes sense to us fully only as we come to be fully transformed by it.* If, like Paul, we enter into relationship with God through Christ, accepting the grace of the cross and experiencing the *metanoia* that it produces, we will find that the message can be understood only in the process of living it out. We are *in process of transformation*—not yet perfected but no longer without a glimpse of what that perfection will be. The Spirit has set us free from the law of sin and death, however long the mental and spiritual habit of slavery may seem to persist. Having been set free, however, it is time for us to exert our freedom to set out on pilgrimage. As we live our pilgrimage in quest of understanding, the Word of God in Scripture will challenge and unsettle and prod us onward. For it unveils its mysteries only to the pilgrim; and only when we are perfectly transformed shall we understand them perfectly.

Epilogue

Perhaps the greatest enemy of a true reading of Scripture is simply a false estimate of what the Bible really is. Having accepted the Bible, in the early stages of our Christian profession, as true and authoritative, we are likely to misconceive what that means. We may well suppose that for the Bible to be true and authoritative, it must utter the last word on every possible topic. It comes as a shock to us, then, to realize that the Bible contains errors of science and history and also, what is worse, contradictions in matters of belief and morality.

One response to this discovery is to close one's eyes to it. Much of American Christianity has done exactly that. Fundamentalists and some others who claim the venerable name of Evangelicals simply insist that the Bible is everything that the unreflective believer might wish it to be. Yet the Bible itself does not bear these claims out. In such a situation, the reflective person will have to decide between a fundamentalist notion of what the Bible should be and the facts of what the Bible is. If our belief in Scripture as the Word of God is genuine, it is clear that we must decide in favor of the Bible itself rather than our own theological preferences.

I have argued here that we should not ignore the fallibility of Scripture but should understand it as inevitable if God is to communicate with us in this created universe, where we are all bound to the limitations of time and space. The Word of God cannot *be* God, but that does not make it less valuable to us. It can be an authority for us by giving us a sense of identity and hope, some norms of belief and behavior, and even some checks on our performance. Yet written words are too limited to do this once and for all. Human life changes; and authority must be living, too, if it is to function in every age.

Under God, who alone is absolute, Bible and Christian community work together to provide us with a living authority. They influence one another, for the Bible is a product of the community of faith, and the task of interpreting it falls largely to that community. Since the community accepts the Scriptures as its charter, it can never escape from their judgment. The church is not unchanging, and it needs the Bible to help it find its bearings as it moves and grows. The Bible, on the other hand, was created in past eras, and it requires the work of interpretation in order to speak to a later day.

The words of Scripture come to us from ages past and recount God's dealings with people whose experience is likely to have been worlds away from ours. Yet the very remoteness of Scripture opens our eyes to see that God may deal with humanity in many ways other than the ones we ourselves have encountered. There is a kind of dangerous contentment with the present—or at least a willingness to stay caught in it—that is the greatest possible barrier to our becoming what God intends for us. Scripture breaks through that barrier, showing that there is more to know and do and be—and so opens our eyes to the distant goal.

The Christian pilgrimage to the New Jerusalem is a journey that begins here but travels further. To become what God wants us to be means that we shall have to become more than we are at this moment. Scripture prompts us to *metanoia,* the recognition of where we are and the desire to go on toward the goal. There is no better means that God could have given for the purpose. By drawing us outside our own narrow boundaries, God shows us how desirable are the farther horizons.

God speaks to us through the Word of Scripture. Yet as we have seen, it is not always easy to hear what God is saying. The difficulties arise from the limitations of human speech, of writing, of our created nature (which prohibits any kind of static perfection), and also from our own unreadiness to hear. Reading and listening to the Bible, then, calls for knowledge, skill, and devotion. Our reward is to be freed for the pilgrim journey.

Trinity Press International, Valley Forge, is an independent, ecumenical publisher whose goal is to create a strong and vigorous literature, predominantly within the Christian tradition, that will enlighten and quicken religious thought and action throughout the world. The Press therefore provides serious and accessible books in theology for a broad range of readers within and outside the church that address the deepest questions human beings ask, and that assist in the formation of an intelligent, moral, and effective faith community of the future.

Cowley Publications is a ministry of the Society of St. John the Evangelist, a religious community for men in the Episcopal Church. Emerging from the Society's tradition of prayer, theological reflection, and diversity of mission, the press is centered in the rich heritage of the Anglican Communion.

Cowley Publications seeks to provide books, audio cassettes, and other resources for the ongoing theological exploration and spiritual development of the Episcopal Church and others in the body of Christ. To this end, it is dedicated to developing a new generation of theological writers, encouraging them to produce timely, creative, and stimulating publications of excellence, and making these publications available widely, reaching both clergy and lay persons.